The Conversation of

The Conversation of

Venusta

A Sequel to *The Conversation of Merachefet*

by

C. JoyBell C.

www.cjoybellc.com
authorcjoybellc@gmail.com

Feb 2018

To Flore

With deep Love, enjoy the journey
Any journey. Ale xxx

This is for The Brave, This
is for The True, This is for
The Seeker, The Sage,
The Pure.

This is indeed for you

:)

Introduction

My work of this particular nature can be described by many terms, such as, Philosophy of Mind, Mysticism, Esotericism, Hermetics, Soul Alchemy, Theurgy, and I'm sure there are several more terms out there that I'm not even fully acquainted with. I suppose though, the most important term would be the concept by which you and I choose to identify my work. What do you feel my work is, to you? Then let me stop to ponder and ask the same question, of myself.

I guess I tend to identify my work by how it affects others who receive it. *The Conversation of Merachefet*, to which *The Conversation of Venusta* is a sequel, was a book that I almost did not publish. I hesitated with a festering hesitation! I considered it very esoteric, probably too esoteric for people to deal with. But then, I thought, regardless of the outcome — regardless of how it would be received by people — maybe the important thing was that those for whom it was meant, could access it. I gradually came to see that it didn't really matter if, let's say, half of the people who read it didn't get it; but, what mattered is that the other half *would* get it, and if they really got it, their lives would probably be changed forever.

I always say that it is not my mission to change lives; but let's be real here, if my work wasn't changing lives, then I wouldn't be motivated to do it. I really do not write for fame. Of course, I am very grateful and thankful for the fame that comes along with it. Why? Well because, if I am to write my name upon the skies as I do, then I better write it repeatedly, attached to many life-changing and world-shaking words that transform the hearts and minds of people, everywhere! Because I know that to write your name upon a human heart, is to write your name upon Eternal Stone. So why not make it many human hearts, from everywhere and all over?

So I guess we can identify what I do as, "life-changing work", and for that I am very grateful. I am grateful that anyone, anywhere, reads the things that I write. I am today very pleased that I made the right decision of publishing *The Conversation of Merachefet*, and I am surprised to say that it is my most highly-rated book, so far! Perhaps it came at a time when—though I thought that people would not be ready for it— people were in fact *very* ready! And, maybe just maybe, it is what they were actually waiting for! I have since received the most astonishing feedback from readers of *Merachefet*, from stories of how the book makes them burst into spontaneous gales of laughter and tears; to stories of how I must be a Prophetess for I have written the "most profound work" that they "have ever had the pleasure of reading"! This feedback alone denotes that readers *do* understand my esoteric work, and that they *do* in fact need it!

Gathering from feedback I've received so far, I think I can safely say that you believe my work is profound and magical; I will therefore go with those terms to describe it. But, what is "profound + magical"? When you ask yourself that simple question, that is the time when you are faced with all those very lofty terms that I enumerated at the beginning of this introduction, because they are all words to describe the profoundly magical, or, the magically profound.

Initially the title of this book was, *Whereabouts of Soul;* however, it just so happens that while writing it, I came into communication with the head and founder of the modern day societies of the Roman Pagan nations: *Nova Roma*, *Byzantium Novum*, and *The Julian Society*, who told me that I am the Living Incarnation of the Goddess Venus. They have in fact instated me as the Goddess, amongst themselves. Now, whether or not we believe in myths and gods and such, this is nevertheless a delightful honour; one which I thought would be worth honouring in return, by reflecting onto the title of this book. You are not required to believe in such things, in order to appreciate the novelty of the whole scenario.

"Venusta" is the Latin word that embodies all the attributes of Venus: Love, Lust and Beauty. It was once written of me that I might be the incarnate of Athena, a fact that can be attested in my book #2 *Vade Mecum* (see the foreword written there by Joe Puglia). When people think of my work, they think of Wisdom, which is of course attributed to Athena; but, when delving into the nature of my work, one will find that the heart of my work has to do with Venusta (the attributes of Beauty, Love and all things that decorate a Beautiful Life). But its meaning is even more elaborate than that: while "venusta" is a word derived from the name of a Goddess, it is at the very same time a word that was put to use for everyday description of attractiveness, decoration, etcetera. I like the symbolism of this word, in that it embodies the Divine in everyday life, it is the golden necklace that is worn every day, the diamond ring that is never taken off. It is the precious treasure that goes with you always.

Furthermore, I also saw the connection between how I initially wanted to entitle my first book, (*Merachefet*), as *The Conversations of Venus.* Then it just fell into place like pieces in a puzzle and it made more sense to entitle this book as I have.

For the book cover design, I wanted it to really express the essence of the book's contents. The roses and the lilies express the duality found within the book and I believe they express the ongoing conversation. The lilies want to learn from the roses, want to become the roses; but at the same time, the two are one in the same. I was blessed to be able to work with a photographer who could grasp my vision and make it his own. The haze of misty color and sparkle that you can see in the background is actually a superimposition of Aurora Borealis! The Northern Lights is something of magical significance to me, and even for those who do not really believe in magic or even in the existence of their own souls, the Aurora

Borealis does not fail to leave any mind in awe of its workings! I wanted to add it to my cover, to permanently encapsulate the nature and the message of it, which in turn brings the whole design into fruition.

In my introduction to *Merachefet* I explained how these "conversations" are something that I see as a dialogue between Soul and Mind; between my Higher Self and my Mundane Self; between Inner and Outer. I freely exchange knowledge with my Mundane Self on a daily basis and this constitutes the dialogue that has now become a book series. I also explained in my previous introduction, how the dialogue is the root of my writing process, the root of how I am able to bring my so many words to the banqueting table for all of you to dine on. It all starts from a place that I am uncovering for the rest of you, here in this book and in the previous one.

Something you will notice while reading my books of conversation, is that there are certain words capitalized at certain times during the conversation.

The reason why I continue to do this, is to signify divinity and/or importance. In order to distinguish between the mundane form and the Higher Form.

The Conversation of Venusta is a work that I truly believe everyone should become fluent in. If *Merachefet* was a book that I sent out into the world not being a hundred percent sure of publishing; this time, I can say that I am a hundred percent sure that everyone should read this one. In fact, I will hold onto a copy of this book for me to read and re-read over and over again, as I know this is my Higher Voice answering the questions of my Mundane Mind, and oh, if only I could always remain in my Higher State at all times! I guess I can, if I really want to and if I really embrace my Inner Nature. I think I will do just that!

I want to formally welcome you into the pages of a book containing a long conversation between Inner and Outer, between Lesser and Higher, between Angel and Human, between Goddess and Girl. I can honestly say that you will learn so much more and I can truthfully say that I am actually a little frightened! I am frightened because I feel like I go through experiences in life that I really don't need to experience, at all, but I only experience them for the sake of writing this series of books for all of you! A sacrificial lamb, per se. So, that is why I am a little frightened. Allow me to just declare here, that I don't agree with being a 'sacrificial lamb' on behalf of the world, on behalf of you, or of anyone. I certainly will not gauge my eye out for you as Odin did! Although, I feel that many times, I already did gauge my eyes out during painful and hurtful experiences, which unveiled to me the Wisdom that I herein reveal. However, I *do not* see those experiences as 'payments' to gain something in return; rather, I see those experiences as avenues taken to be able to have the right to stand upon my teachings with utmost conviction, because I, having first lived them, *do* know them by heart! They are mine through and through!

Along with the release of this book, I also release myself from future sacrifices that would be expected of me in order to lead and to teach others. May anything that I teach in the future, be only lessons brought about by Joy, by Laughter, only by Illuminated Dreams at night.

Maybe it is only our minds that believe we must endure and suffer in order to gain, so that we may give. Perhaps it is only our own minds that are at error! I would like to put an end to this. May we gain from Laughter, may we gain from Beauty, may we gain from Happiness, may we gain from Mercy, from Abundance, from Gratitude, from Limitless Resources! May we gain through good and not through bad, and from this well of Abundance, may we share with others! And it is with this final blessing that I invite you to turn the last page of the introduction, and begin The Conversation. Thank you so much for being here right now, to read what I have written.

"The heavenly does not only surround us during our innocent childhood, but at any moment of our lives; we just don't know it yet or any more. Beyond the person we think we are, is a second person, whom we do not see: our real or 'higher' Self already existing before thoughts and desires took hold of us. Beyond our body of flesh and blood lives a radiant and sublime consciousness. Our true life flows in the depth of our heart and is not part of the superficial mask of the personality which we show to the world. Student on the Path, you are heir to a treasure hidden deep down in the recesses of your own nature: 'The Kingdom of Heaven is within you.'"— Rosae Crucis

"Tell me, how can I find myself, how can I find all of me? You already taught me how to find myself, I know that, but how can I find the very last pieces of me, even the ones I've forgotten about?"

"They have told you that in order to be happy and to be whole, you must not seek for another to fulfill you, you must not seek for another to fulfill voids in you and to complete you; but I tell you that they know not of what they speak. There are in fact places within your Soul that are locked up, because another person holds the key to them. When you find that person, when they find you, that is when you must let the person unlock the gates for you, unlock the doors and the spaces that they hold the keys to.

We were not born into this world to be alone and to not find fulfillment in another. If there was to be no fulfillment found in another, then there would be no reason to come down here, in the first place. Sometimes you are following someone else on the way down here and other times, someone is following you... I am sure that there are those who follow no one and whom no one follows; they have their own paths to take; but to say that they are the standard is a falsity, it is a lie.

We find a set of wings in ourselves, on our own, but we find another set of wings in another, a pair that we could never find alone! To say that you are whole and that you are full all on your own, is a great arrogance! It is a lack of humility. Like I already said, perhaps this is true for some; but this is certainly not true for all. No matter how much you want to never need another, you will always need another. You need a family, you need to belong, you need to have a pack that you can call your own. Sometimes, that pack is found in only one or two people; other times, it is found in a whole bunch of them! But most likely, we find different things in different people, and yet, there is that one other whom our soul seeks to find, because there is a void without them, because that void is the part of you that they fit into. And their void is the part of them that you fit into.

We are all needy and beautiful at the same time. It is the culture of our day and age to teach and to learn how *not* to be 'needy', how *not* to be 'clingy', how *not* to end up being 'shortchanged' in love and in life in general. It is the current prevalent societal norm, to seek to teach and to master how to never need, or at least how to never show it! We cast aside those with whom we become closer to, on the basis of us feeling like they are 'needy', we condemn them and call them 'desperate', 'uncool', 'clingy'… the moment there is a desire to maintain and to grow in closeness and in bond, it is too often met with disdain and rejection from the other end. People today buy books that teach them how to manipulate someone else into loving them, they buy books that teach them how to detach, how to be 'alpha male' or 'alpha female'. People of the world today, are not living in reality; they are living in a phantasm, an illusion— a world where nobody needs anybody, because everyone is self-generating and self-sufficient. In that illusion of a world, the moment people are born, they begin to eat and walk and clothe themselves, all on their own! And when people die in that land of illusions, they bury themselves and they kiss themselves goodbye, they buy their own coffins and drain their own blood out of their own bodies! You see? They are born and die with no needs! They don't need anybody, not anyone! They need no relationships, they need no love, they need nobody, nobody at all! But that is in the land of unreality, you see, and we don't live in that land. In our reality, we are born in need and we die in need; therefore, there is no point in trying to escape the fact that we *are* needy, because we come from need and we return to need!

From the very day you are born into this world, you are in need of love, of attention, and of care. From the moment you are conceived, you are in need of a healthy womb to be conceived and to grow in. When you are already born, and as you grow, you are completely helpless and at the mercy of others around you, until such a time that you are big enough, strong enough and capable enough of taking care of yourself and providing for yourself. But you fool yourself if you think that once you reach that age of maturity, there is nothing else that you are needy of! You think that you are not in need of love, attention, care, and of affection? Do you think that all needs are physical? Because if that is what you think, then you are gravely wrong. You will always have that need to belong, to have people to come home to, to be remembered in the hearts and the minds of those who hold you dear to them. Even those who profess no need for any affections have a very strong need for revenge, for dominance and for power. And in this reality that we live in, when a person dies, that person cannot self-sufficiently prepare his burial, dig his grave, light his candles and position himself inside of his coffin. In the reality that we live in, a person who dies is completely void of self, completely dependent on the mercies, the good graces and the love, of those around him. In both birth and death, we are in need of love. Why is there any time and any thoughts spent on the idea that as we live our lives, we are to strive to need no one, to love ourselves independently of others, and to seek everything that we need and want, within ourselves? Why is there even a thought given towards that? It is unrealistic and it is born of illusion. It is born of the imagination of belonging to some other world wherein love is not necessary.

Perhaps the whole notion of needlessness is born from pain and fear— pain and fear being the biological parents of this illusion. It is no hidden truth that we are so often hurt by those who are responsible for caring for us, which leaves us wounded, scarred, and afraid. Perhaps there are so many wounds, so many scars, too many for anyone to deal with! So instead of finding a root that produces the balm to heal this malaise, we have produced in its place a quick-acting band-aide solution! Kind of like fast food!

Because we have crafted a society wherein nobody has the time or the motivation to cook good meals at home, we invented fast food which isn't good for anybody. In this same light, we teach and learn that all we will ever need is inside of us, because 'we are the universe', and because 'we are self-sufficient'. We teach and we learn that 'neediness' is a sign of weakness, anyway, so wipe your tears, pick yourself up, and go out and fuck everyone you want, because relationships are not even important, anyway. We are 'just animals', anyway, who need to 'get our fix'. What a handy solution we have come up with, an answer to the brokenness of the human soul— more brokenness! I suppose the logic behind it is this: 'if you can't fix the broken vase, then just break it some more!'

We are all needy and we are all beautiful, and the only two types of people in the world are the people who are brave enough to accept that they are needy, and the people who are *not* brave enough to accept that they are needy (or who have been conditioned for so long into believing that nobody should ever find out about their neediness). We are beautifully needy, and if all of us were to accept that, then all of us would have so much more understanding, acceptance and compassion for ourselves and for other people.

Are you afraid of getting hurt? Afraid of pain? *Pain is just another feeling,* which, at the end of one's life, will really not matter any more than all of the other feelings that you have shared with the people or with the person that you have loved in life! At the grave, there is no place for finding pain in the ways that you gave too much; there will only be room for finding pain in the ways that you didn't give enough, that you didn't receive enough, and in the ways that you refused, you doubted, you ran away. Is it typical of you to run away? Where is the honour in running away? Are you ashamed of loving someone too much? There is no shame in love! Even when you happen to have loved someone not worthy of your love, *remember this— that the value of another person (their worth and their quality), can never alter or dictate the value (the worth and the quality) of your own love for them. Only you determine the value of your own love. It is only you who can do that!* There is no shame in love, and there is no shame in being loved. But there is much shame in cowardice and in fear. There is much shame in doubt and in vengeance. There is definitely no shame in believing that there is someone who may truly fill the part of you that is empty, that waits, that longs.

This is not about being idealistic and it is not about reading romances in books and wishing that we had the same; but this is about the truth of the matter, that you may spend every single day with

someone who is supposed to fill you, who is *supposed*
to *be* the other half of you, and yet, they simply do
not fit into you! Who would want that? Who would
ask for such a life? Who would want to love someone
while longing for another whom they have not even
met? A longing for something that you know not,
and yet, you *do* know it more than anything else!
Nobody asks for this desire, nobody asks for this
void, nobody asks to yearn like this! Nobody would
want that! And yet, it is there! Even though there is
someone already there who is supposed to fill it! You
may be living the most ideal scenario that anyone
could imagine, and still wake up at night, startled in
the dawn hours, looking to the window, calling out
to a name you don't even know, so that he or she
may come find you! Who would want that? Nobody
would want that!

The fact is that there are those whom we seek.
We remember them somehow, and we look for
them. But there is one who knows us well, they
carry the keys to us, to unlock us, and that is the one
we ought to spend the rest of our lives with.

Many people think that love represents chains,
bondage, the opposite of freedom. But people who

believe such things are simple-minded creatures who have been lied to, and who easily accept the general trend of the lie. It is in fact love that is the only thing powerful enough to set one free from even the most deeply-embedded and thoroughly-wound chains of the soul, the mind and the body. The fact is that we are born into chains and born into bondages; these things are put upon us by fear, pain and doubt. When you are thoroughly loved by someone in mind and in heart, this has the power to set you so free, more free than you have ever been before. And that is because freedom is not the equivalent of detachment. Freedom is the equivalent of that which sets you free. And when someone loves you the way that only they can, *that* is what sets you free! The one who loves you does not chain you! The one who loves you carries the keys to setting you free, carries the keys to opening your gates and opening your doors."

"Why do we let someone else keep those keys? Why don't we just keep them, ourselves? Wouldn't it be easier to keep the keys to yourself, by your side, instead of giving them to another?"

"I believe we let another one keep our keys, so that we will know it is really them when they find us again. When only one person holds those keys, then it can only be the one and none other than the one!"

"They've told me that I should be the Captain of my own Ship, the CEO of my own life; they told me that I should be quick to remove anyone who doesn't lift me up the highest I can go! At the very first signs of adversity I should leave, that is what they told me!"

"Yes, I have heard what they say about leaving someone the moment they 'show you who they are'; about removing people from your life the very moment that they show a single sign of rudeness, of meanness or the like. As if everyone is good enough to dump anyone at the first sign of a flaw! Why, are you flawless? Are any of us flawless? The only person who may be at liberty to remove another person from their life at the first sign of a flaw is the person who himself has no flaw! Go ahead, if you have no meanness and no rudeness in you at all, then you may feel free to remove anyone who shows you any signs of these!

The problem with that kind of thinking lies in the fact that many people do not know who they are yet, they are still finding themselves; just like you, and not unlike you, they have times of clouded mind, wherein they feel lost within the turmoil and the typhoons of past hurts and fears, they cannot think clearly, they cannot function properly, and it is in these exact moments that a true friend will stay and will pull his friend out from the mental hurricane that he is stuck into! It is in times like these that a friend is in fact a friend! That a lover is in fact a lover! Do you think that it stands as evidence against a person when they are flung into their moments of imperfection? No. Nothing else is expected of a person other than to be their imperfect selves! Why? Do you expect more? Then you yourself must first be perfect, in that case! But what this does is that it stands as evidence about *you*— if you are the one who cannot stand there for an imperfect lover, an imperfect mate, an imperfect friend— then what kind of a person are *you?*

As a matter of fact, many times we will meet diamonds that are covered in mud! Actually, diamonds are from the earth, stuck in mud, under layers of useless chunk of rock and dirt. All real diamonds are! Do we judge a diamond based upon how many layers of mud and guck it used to be stuck under? Or do we judge a diamond based upon its value as a diamond? Then why should it be any different from a person? Tell me why! You have no answer, because there is none!

Many people find their soulmates still stuck in the mud, like diamonds, but instead of digging them out of the mud and polishing them, they opt to go for popular opinion and leave the muddy diamond behind. They opt to see the flaws and say, 'You're not adding anything to my life, I will now remove you' and in doing so, they have lost a perfect diamond in the rough, one that *was* meant for them. And in losing that, they alter the course of their lives.

The key to failure is the expectation of flawlessness. Circumstances are flawed, situations are flawed, people are flawed, experiences are flawed... things do not need to be untouched by the muddy hands of imperfection in order to be worthwhile. There is no such thing as untouched. What there is, is strength, tenacity, belief... unhappiness is fleeting and anger is shallow, the wise soul does best in looking beyond these and staying true to himself and to others, not because they and he are perfect, but because value is not measured in imperfection and perfection. Value is measured by how much you are willing to give in order to have something. Or to keep it.

Yes, of course, it is entirely possible and it does happen, that some people become spoiled with too much kindness and too much understanding; and in such cases, it is needful to withdraw your energies from the person who has been spoiled by your affections. We may withdraw ourselves on the basis that we have given more than what a person can handle healthfully; not on the basis that they are flawed. It is indeed a sad circumstance that people can be spoiled with understanding and affections… kindness is taken for granted… this is different from being myred, this is different from having flaws! One who takes things for granted displays a lack of gratitude, and a lack of gratitude is not simply a flaw; but this is a state of being that is characteristic of a different type of soul. Still, even the ungrateful have hope to change; however, that hope must not become your responsibility in the least."

"Have you ever left anyone? And if so, why did you leave them?"

"I was once very close in heart to a man whose friendship I later dissolved completely. He twisted my mind in ways that I'm afraid have truly damaged me. Or not. I am a fast healer. But he twisted my mind and I participated in the twisting by letting him stay in my life. Thankfully, it was only for a year and then the friendship was over.

That man would reach up to me, in order to pull me down. But I didn't know this at the time, because at the time, I thought that I was the one who needed to reach up higher, because his communication with me led me to believe that I wasn't good enough, wasn't beautiful enough, wasn't smart enough, wasn't attractive enough. He achieved his goal by constantly uplifting every other woman around me, whilst simultaneously withholding anything good that he could tell me about myself. But he would appreciate me every once in a while— he was training me like a man trains a horse— placing little bits of apples in my mouth every now and then, whenever he was able to put me in the place he wanted me to be, and that place was at level with him and at level with those women whom he knew he could easily have. It was a manipulative tactic like those used on animals, and I find it very unfortunate that it was ever used on me.

It took me a year to realise that I was not the one who needed to reach up; but that I was in fact the one who was constantly lowering herself to gain the approval of a man who was beneath her. No man will need to pull you down unless he is already beneath you. No man will need to lift up everyone around you to make you feel like you have no advantage as a person, unless he is aware that you are in fact better than they are, that you are better than what he can actually have.

That actually happened to me twice, with two different men, each lasting a year before I woke up. I don't know why it took a year of sleep for me to wake up each time, but now I know for certain that I will never fall into that sleep, ever again.

I am in fact too much like Cinderella, and there are many, many people in this world that are in fact too much like Cinderella's stepsisters and stepmother. I suppose that there are other Cinderellas out there, too, girls who believe that they must give up what they have in order to appease the malevolent. *Maybe if I give them all of this, they will appreciate me; Maybe if I give up all of that, they will appreciate me; Maybe if I do this for them or that for them, they will love me...* but the malevolent character of man and of woman, is not, and will never be, appeased by acts of kindness. This is something that I want you to always remember. There are attittudes that are capable of change; but there are also character traits that will never, ever change. One cannot change the color of one's soul. Envy dyes the color of the soul a pitch black, and that is a color of soul that will never change. Even those who wish they could be with you, can in fact envy you, due to the fact that they are aware that you are quite unreachable. Do not ever mistake desire of attainment for affection. One may desire to attain you, not out of love and not out of affection, but out of the mere wish to conquer you. Stay away from these types of souls, avoid these kinds of people."

"Does this envy that you speak of exist in other ways and in other areas of life, as well?"

"Of course! There are so many people in the world who would wish that no castles existed, because they do not live in castles, themselves. There are many who wish to tear all castles down! You must *know* as a fact, that if you do have more and if you *are* more, there will always be those people who will want to take away from you and who will try to detract of you. It is an immediate given. You must know this, you must be aware of this, because there will always be those who will wish to clip your wings, who will wish to burn your home, who will wish to set your body on fire.

Love the people who will help you build your castle, love the people who will help you make your home, love the people who protect you. Then stay away from those who don't."

"But what if I can't stay away from the malevolent and the envious? What if I must be with them, due to circumstance? Then what do I do?"

"You may always remove yourself in your soul and mind. To be with someone or with some people is not always a state of the body! To be with someone or with some people is often a state of the mind, of the soul. You may learn to remove yourself in soul by the removal of reactive attachments to such people. You may learn to remove yourself in mind, by removing your eagerness to belong. I know that we all need to belong and I know that we all *must* belong, but be patient, my love, be patient. Be patient my darling, be patient. You will arrive at a place of belongingness; it will take time, but that time will come."

"Is it important to stay away in mind and in soul? Is it truly important to avoid them?"

"My dear, it is more important than you realise. It is very, very important. You are a wildflower, you see, untouched by the prying eyes of envy, untouched by the filthy hands of greed; that is what it means to be a wildflower out in the wild under the Sun and with the Winds and the Sky! You are pure. But then you let someone cut you and put you in a vase, only to wither and to be thrown out to the trash in a few days— why do you do this? Do not do this! One day, they will all wither and they will all fade away, and you will still remain, a wildflower! Untouched, unblemished, unfaded— that will be you. Only the hands of protection may touch you, only the eyes of affection and admiration may gaze. Let them fade away, may you remain eternal."

"I have heard it said before, that you will know who the 'right one' is, by the ease of acquiring happiness in the relationship. They say that if it all comes easily, with no effort, then that means the person is the 'right one'. I want you to tell me what you think about this statement. Is it true? Is it false? Tell me what you think!"

"This statement is true when applied to those who are mundane, but in the realm of Gods, Angels and Demons, this statement is merely food for dull minds down below. If right equaled easy, then there would be no need for Warriors and for Angels! The truth is that sometimes the right person is wrapped in hell and you are wrapped in hell; but you are each others' Warriors, you are each others' Angels, you are the ones who can unwrap one another! Some of the best people are those covered in the worst scars and possessing the strongest of hearts. Now, if you are going to dismiss a person like that, on mere basis that it is not easy and therefore it is not 'right' for you, then you may very well be missing out on the greatest Love of your life, the greatest accomplishment of your life, and the most magnificent person that you were to ever know. Of course, I am not saying that all who come wrapped up in hell must be worked on, but, what I am saying is that, if Michelangelo did not toil to free the Angels that he saw so imprisoned in the marble rocks in front of him, then we would have no Angels of marble stone in the Sistine Chapel, today. If Michelangelo did not toil to free David from the marble he was confined in, then the mighty David would not be standing in Florence today. Michelangelo saw them in the stone, and he carved until he set them free. And that is precisely why I say, that this does not apply to those who are mundane, and that is because, not all are Michelangelos! Michelangelo belongs to the realm of God, Angel and Demon. If you are not among his ranks, then do not try to carve the marble! You will inevitably fail! In the first place, you will not even see the Angel within the stone, and therefore,the statement you asked of me would apply to you in such a case. But only in that case. So you see, the statement you asked of me *does* apply to those not of the ranks of Michelangelo, but to those of us who are— that statement is an error and a failure. We see the Angels in the marble, and we carve until we set them free!

It is interesting, by the way, how people normally see Love as something that does not set them free; but rather, does just the opposite of that! But that is false. Love is the Angel in the marble, and it cannot thrive until it has been set free! Love toils for itself and it frees itself, too! If I Love the Angel in the marble slab that only I can see, I carve until the stone has wings and can dance and can breathe and can Love me as I Love it! Love cannot breathe until it has been set free, you see, and it is Love that sets Love free! There is all Freedom in Love! All Freedom! You must in fact be so Free, in order to bind yourself to another! It is Freedom so felt and so experienced that allows us the ability to bind ourselves to another. To be bound in Love is in fact the fruit of Ultimate Freedom."

"What do you think about divorce? Because there are so many of those who believe that one must never divorce someone whom they promised the rest of their lives to. To do so would be a sin! What do you think of this bondage? Is marriage the ultimate bond of Freedom and of Love? And if we seek to break it, under any circumstance, would that be a transgression against that ultimate bond?"

"To answer that question, I need you to imagine yourself floating above our planet, floating above the

Earth. Go ahead, float above the Earth, in the dark cosmos, and look down at it from above— there it is, a blue dot with green patches— now think of the human race, think of all the people living on that planet. Some of those people have gathered together and formed governments in order to dictate all of the other people around them, and these governments give permission to billions of people so that they may love one person for the rest of their lives and so that they may legally bring children into the world, together. Now, out of those billions of people, many of them believe that God has ordained them to stay together, no matter what, come what may, and that if they were to ever part ways, that would be the ultimate transgression and shame of their lives. Marriage, to many, is a way of shutting their eyes to any other possibilities that Destiny may have in store for them, and for these people, a marriage gone sour is an entire Destiny collapsed!

It *is* in fact Love that is the ultimate Freedom and the ultimate Bondage, and when I say Bondage here, I do not mean anything negative at all. It is a beautiful Bondage that dictates you will find one another again and again and again, throughout many lifetimes. That cannot in any way be compared to bondages of the mundane, the ones that pull and hold them down.

When you have become so hurt and so pained by the one you have pledged your life to, it is time to see that Destiny has something more in store for you. We often believe that pain is the signal of an end, but nay, pain is the signal of a new beginning! That is why there is pain at birth— because it is a new beginning, a new life, a new realm altogether. When there is so much pain inflicted upon you, so much negligence and harshness, this is something you must let go of, regardless of marriage contracts! Destiny is showing you a new path, a new way; fight for a marriage for as long as the marriage also fights for you! Now, remember that! I will say it again: *Fight for a marriage for as long as the marriage fights for you!*

Carve out the Angel for as long as the Angel's heart still beats! Why do you think that Michelangelo has many half-carved slabs of marble? Only a half of an angel, only a half of a wing… it is because the heart inside stopped beating! It is because the wing inside stopped flapping! And that is the time that he put down his chisel. This is also the time that you must put down your promise and end the relationship you once pledged your life to. Do you think that Michelangelo would pick up his chisel without an intention to complete the Angel? Of course not! Why then even pick up the chisel, in the first place? But with each marble slab he was given and with each chisel that he held up to stone— he carved with full intention to see his vision come to full term fruition. Sometimes, heartbeats stop and wings fail, despite our strongest intentions, so we must know when to put down our chisels. And when we do put down our chisels for the dying marble Angels, we must turn our faces towards elswhere, and we must begin to carve our Davids and our Sistine Chapels!"

"And what about kindness with referrence to the rest of the world, not with referrence to Love and to Soulmates? Surely, all things are applicable to their own areas of common sense, which makes me now wonder, how are we to be kind to the world and to all of its inhabitants? How are we to choose whom to give to, whom to be kind to? Who is going to understand our kindness and who is not going to understand it?"

"You are right to believe that kindness is a language, and just like any other language, some understand it and some do not. We each speak our own language, and even in our kindness, this comes out in different languages, as well."

"Did I even mention that I think kindness is likened unto language?"

"You didn't mention it, but that's what you were thinking, was it not?"

"Yes, I was thinking that! But please explain to me what you have just told me."

"In order to explain this, let me tell you a story about cats!"

"About cats?"

"Yes, about cats! You see, I once took a stray cat from off the street, she would come around to the house and she was always pregnant! I started giving her food and calling her *Allessandra*. She had litter after litter of kittens, most of which all perished, but after some time of being fed well and treated well, she finally had a beautiful litter of kittens that survived. All left, went off early on into their kittenhood, leaving just one orange cat, whom I have named Kuchen. Kuchen is a cat ever-so-gentle, far more gentle than most people I have met. He is now bigger than his mother, Alessandra, but he still considers her before doing all things. He won't even eat until she has first eaten the best parts of their home-cooked meals, and when his sibling and their friend fight him off, he will bow his head and willingly turn away. Yet, he always takes the opportunity to show the others his affections for them, by rubbing up against their bodies and twirling his tail around theirs whenever he can. He doesn't want tension, he doesn't want any type of negative energy around him, and he attempts to diffuse it with his gentleness and affections. It is a very remarkable thing to behold!"

"Tell me more! Who are Kuchen's sibling and friend?"

"Yes, Kuchen has a smaller sibling from a different litter and there is a friend who attaches himself to their little family unit, a friend who is not from around where we are, but who comes around for the meals. He watches them while they rub against each other and intertwine their tails around one another's tails. Sometimes, I think he knows he is an outsider and he never really warms up totally, but at the same time, he is very meak and gentle towards the others and towards me. Kuchen's little sibling, whom I simply call, 'Little Pretty', is something like a small feline princess who was born into an already established family of well-placed former street cats (since I took Alessandra in from the streets and she has had offspring here and they have been raised by me, this is now their home and they are now 'locals', no longer strangers.) Of the whole bunch, Kuchen is the closest to me, because it is he whom I favoured since he was born, and it is he who is the most gentle and most affectionate and selfless in nature and in deed. He truly astounds me!"

"Tell me all about these cats. Tell me more about them!"

"Well, now that you can see the picture of the cats, I can tell you the rest of the story. There have come around here a great number of street cats. I guess they have some sort of feline communication and somehow, it was revealed to others that there is food available here for a few lucky cats. So, later on, they all began pouring in! Very hostile, loud cats contrary to the nature of Alessandra when I first found her outside my door. The other strays are just loud, hostlie, malicious and self-serving. They come here because they know of the comforts, but they do so with self-service in mind. Yes, I understand that they have come in here from a hostile world where they are perhaps kicked and spit upon, they dodge cars in order not to get run over, they have bald patches on their bodies and fierce gazes in their eyes, and I understand why. I know of their circumstances out there in their own world, outside of our gated yard, so, it is therefore very difficult for me to now turn them away; but I really must! I must turn them away, and I must use force to do so in order to counteract their relentlessness! And just like Kuchen, I would rather not have to fight them away, I would rather simply turn away and hope for the best, but alas, to do so is to turn one's face away from reality and away from the home bred cats and their home here. I would be doing a true disservice towards the cats for whom I have affections if I were to only turn a blind eye to the hostile and aggressive natures of the intruders. It would even be a disservice to myself, for in doing so, I disrespect the effort that I have given to feed and to raise these goods cats in a loving environment. They come in over our gates and they fight off my native cats every feeding time! They attack Alessandra, Kuchen, Little Pretty, and their friend. They snarl, they hiss, they scratch and they raise all hairs on their bodies just to intimidate the others! And so my own cats end up not being able to eat! Little Pretty fights back, but Kuchen, Alessandra, and their friend, never get to eat more than a bite when the intruders are around!

Out of compassion, as well as the desire to avoid having to act out in forceful ways, I have tolerated their behaviour in hopes that they would one day change. But the last straw was when one of the hostile cats attacked *me*! It attacked me and it was in that moment that I realised that these new outsiders would never learn to speak the native language that my own cats speak, they would never be able to adapt to the ways of gentleness, kindness, affection, tolerance and sharing. And they would never be able to do this, because they believe their inherent ways as actions worth respecting, for they come in from a cruel world and they hold onto their ferocious behaviour since it has gotten them through so much before. They will never become like Alessandra, because Alessandra, though coming in from the same place, came in with all gentleness, humility, and respect. She never once hissed, never once scratched, never once buckled under the hostility of her world. She spoke the language of kindness even before she came into our territory. And then I raised her offspring well.

But these new cats? They would never be able to change their ways! They would kill each other and they would kill my own cats before that would happen! They had such audacity to even attack me! And I am the one feeding them, considering them, looking upon them in hope!

I finally chased the hostiles away, I hosed them down with water and they ran away. They still try to come back and I still fall under the weight of compassion, but in the end I find I must hose them down yet again! I feel like it takes me a long time to learn my lesson, and that lesson is that, we must guard our own, invest in our own, and realise that some will never come to understand the language of kindness. Perhaps they have their own bizarre language of kindness, for example, if one were to attack me, perhaps that is an "act of kindness" towards his fellow hostile 'brother', but that, of course, is not our own language of kindness and reciprocation!

Now, just like this true story of my cats, there are many people who reciprocate in ways that we cannot fathom. A bomb for a shelter, a gun for a bowl of soup. A knife for an open welcome door, a slap for a kiss. That is their language, it is not our own! It is wrong to assume that some things are universal, when there is nothing that is universal when it comes to the human race. There may be a great number of things 'universal' between two people who are destined to be together throughout this lifetime; or between a group of people who are bound by a certain cause; or between a people who are bound by the ties of family and of creed— yes, that exists— but beyond these, nothing is universal, and more often than not, we don't know when we are speaking a universal language or not! Your smile of kindness to someone may very well not mean kindness to him, at all! Your extension of affections to someone, may very well not reciprocate from him what affections normally would reciprocate, at all! It is a fallacy to believe that as a human race there is a

single language that runs deep through us all—
because this is not true. The only binding trait that
we all share, is the fact that we are all different, the
fact that we will all never be the same, the fact that
we are united by the reality that we don't need to be
the same, to look alike, to think alike. People these
days are too preoccupied with forming the entire
world into a single home; but this is hypocrisy! And
this is hypocrisy, because they cannot even do the
same in their own homes, in their own nations, in
their own personal lives! Attend to the World
Within, first! Attend to your family, first! Attend to
your own nation, first! Speak one language within,
before you attempt to teach your language, without!"

"How do you know if something is real?"

"That's easy. Does it change you? Does it form
you? Does it give you wings? Does it give you roots?
Does it make you look back at a month ago and say,
'I am a whole different person right now'? If yes,
then it's real. The evidence of truth and reality, lies
in how much something can touch you, can change

you, even if it's from very far away. Distance is only the evidence of what can be surpassed.

It amazes me to watch people who profess a firm faith in God— those same people— have a total disbelief in other people that are far away. They say a relationship cannot be real if the other person is far away; meanwhile, they believe themselves to have a relationship with a God whom they have never met, never seen, will never see in this lifetime, and whose very existence is disputed by science. Yet they say that they have a relationship with God, they believe in a book that was written thousands of years ago, they follow it, they believe in it, and yet they have such little faith in people, in another person, in the belief that someone far away can be 100% real and that they can share something 100% real with that same person. This is in fact a form of hypoocrisy and this goes to show that their faith in God is not born of a faith within their hearts, rather, their faith in their God is born from indoctrination and familiar opinion of those around them. If they were walking down the road, and the mailman came up to them handing them a letter saying, "I am your God from beyond and I love you", they would of course tear the letter apart, or, laugh out loud at it! Why would they believe in a relationship professed by a person far away whom they have never met before?"

"So you are saying that the religious are hypocrites?"

"I am saying that if you are not ready to believe in a love for a person and of a person, because they are far away from you or because you have not met them before in this lifetime, then your faith in God cannot be seen as a product of your own heart; because you are not able to reflect the same onto other people/ onto another person. You see, true faith is a state of the heart; it is not a belief born from fear or from peer pressure. Faith is something you carry within yourself, and you will inevitably reflect this onto others, onto another person, because, thus is the state of your heart! It is not a planned date to go to church every Sunday, it is not a planned state of being that one can reason with. Faith is an uncontrollable state of affairs within the human mind and heart. Therefore, true faith is made evident in the apparence of this said uncontrollable state of affairs."

"Do you believe that it is possible to truly love another person that you have not yet met in this lifetime?"

"Some of us are born in love! Some of us are born in love with a person that we've loved from long before the point of being born. Do you actually think that the point of all beginning starts at your birth?

You were born in love! You've known someone and loved someone for longer than you have been alive! So, am I saying that is possible? Yes, that is exactly what I am saying. Am I saying that this is the case with you? Yes, this is exactly what I am saying. But am I saying that this is the case with everyone? No, I am not saying that. Many people are newborns and this life is their first beginning, they have never loved before. But you— you have always been looking for the one that you remember, the one whom you *know*. I know you have always been this way."

"Then how does one become faithful? Because now I feel like in order to find the one who holds the missing keys to me, I need to have belief first, I need to have faith first! So how do I become faithful, then?"

"I believe that we traverse this Earth, to find the missing materials that we need, for building our eternal homes in the world that is adjacent to this one. Adjacent and unseen; but not undetectable. Then, during our lives here, we also utilise materials from our eternal space, for using as we build our lives here in our corporeal space. It is a give-and-take relationship. A give-and-take relationship between our bodies and our souls, between our minds and our spirits. There are materials here that are needed there and those are what we harvest whilst being here. But there are also many materials there that are needed here and those are what we pull into our lives while we are here.

I of course do not think that this is being done by everybody, but I believe that this is being done by some. Some know this is what they are doing, while others later on realise this is what they have been doing all along.

'Heaven' is actually a country that we build within ourselves, or that we continue to build. We come from it, and we harvest materials for it while we are here, doing this through sharing our talents with others, and through being dedicated to our relationships in life, through loving others and through strengthening our ability to believe, through our faith. What is faith? Faith is the strength to believe even when believing is a very difficult thing to do! I think that faith is acquired here in this world, because there is no need to have faith in our eternal countries. But here, as we acquire faith in the midst of our hardships, we are begetting unto our eternal countries the strong glue that holds some buildings and some temples together. It is all for the adjacent world that we do this. And yet, we may bring that world into this one, just the same as our voices are the sounds of our souls speaking through our throats; so are our eternal cities and eternal colours the breath that we breathe while in this life. And sometimes, breath materialises in condensation, and even more, in snow! It can be real. All of it can be real. We need not be limited by physical matter; but we may choose what to make into physical matter.

We may choose our realities, mould them, create them, cause them to bloom in front of our eyes.

You will naturally become faithful, as you hold steadfast to achieving the purpose of your being here. You will naturally become faithful, as you seek to know yourself, to change, to grow. Faith is the natural occurrence of believing even when believing is the most difficult thing to do."

"How am I to know if someone or something is worth fighting for in the future? How am I to know whether to hold onto someone or to let them go? When we are not certain of our futures, how are we to know which one is worth fighting for, when, alas, we are fighting for the best for our futures?"

"Our futures are already there. Do you think that you are creating your future now? Nay, your future is there and you are looking back on yourself now, helping yourself to get to the positive future that you desire! You are journeying from the future, to help yourself. This is made evident by the undeniable tug upon your Soul, into the directions that it wishes you to turn to, to follow, to pursue! That is not instinct; that is in fact just yourself, telling yourself which way you must go! That is the future that you have chosen! Of course, there are other futures that exist with you in it, ones that you did not choose, but others laid out for you, and those are made evident in the stumbling blocks that are placed in your way during your pursuit of your heart's desire (your individual free will choice). Follow your choice, follow your free will, work towards something or towards someone, with the knowledge that what you envision is already there, existing in the future.

You may meet someone only once, but lay down everything and fight to be with that person, only to be told that you are crazy, delusional... when in fact, you may very well be fighting to be with the person who is already there in your future, spending the rest of your life with you! You will know it by the peace that you feel when you decide to choose them, and to choose them, and to choose them! Each time you choose the person, overcoming stumbling blocks, fears, challenges and doubts— you will feel that peace— the peace will tell you that you are going into the right direction. What is the right direction? The right direction is the one that is already existing there in the future, the one that is making you happy, that is giving you peace, that is stabilising your mind."

"Do all people have to make such gigantuan leaps of faith, such as you have just explained to me?"

"No, not all people do. In fact, it is often those with great purposes who are called to see things at such great heights, heights so frighteningly high up in the universe, that others are not even aware that they exist! And this is not necessarily a better thing; we often are led to believe that what is higher is always better, what is more lofty is better, when in fact, it is not necessarily that way. Let the one who is born for low-flying, fly low. Let the one who is born to run slower, run slower. Because the one who is born to fly those spine-tingling heights, will not be able to turn his back on it even though he would like to! Some are chosen in a way that they are not capable of turning their backs on, and they must learn and practice these things, because if not, then there is simply no other path for them to take! They must either learn to fly, or fall! There is no low-flying for them! And that is why I say, let he who is born to fly low— fly low. The Spirit will call unto those who are chosen, and they will rise to their designated heights! And those who are not meant to rise to such heights, have their own purposes in their own lives, and make no mistake by judging their purposes and their directions. Let them be.

I told you before, and I will tell you again, that there are those who have blood running through their veins which is the antidote to poisons! Blood that kills and washes away venoms! If you hear about this, commonly enough, you will desire to have this! But one must not desire to have what one was not built to carry. If your load is lighter— delight in that lightness! If your run is slower or shorter— delight in the rest that you are able to experience. Do not race with others, lest you be given their weights and their lengths and their heights, all of which you were not built to know!"

"But what if my blood is like that, too? What if my blood kills poisons? What if my flight is high and frightening? What if my run is fast and long?"

"Then you will just be. And you will struggle and you will climb and you will find! There will be no other choice! In such a case, do not waste even a single drop of your precious time, on judging those who do not share these same things with you! And do not waste even a single second of your time on trying to bring with you those who are not meant to come with you! But if there are those who are meant to come with you— *never* let go of them! Stay, always stay. And ask them to stay, do not be too proud that you do not ask this of them. For a high flight is better flown along with another. A long and fast run is better ran, along with another. And we are creating our ties and we are developing our bonds, with those whom we will take beyond this lifetime, and even on into lifetimes to come!"

"What are the signs that I may see, in order to know that someone is the one worth fighting for? Or are there no signs? But if there are signs to know who is the one worth fighting for, then tell me! Do tell me!"

"There is a sign, yes. There are several signs, yes. You did not think I would only hint at things and then leave you to your business, did you? Nay, I am here to look out for you, I would never leave you stranded like that, my love.

The first sign, is that the one worth fighting for will often come along to you right after a very difficult experience with another, who was never worth fighting for, but whom you believed to be the one! There is a great deceit that is played out, before the worthy ones come along! This great deceit is played out in attempts to keep you from your great and shining future. Especially if it is a very purposeful one, bearing purpose beyond what is commonly and normally known to man. And this may happen not just one time, but it may happen multiple times."

"This sounds very frightening, very hurtful, I am not sure I would wish for a very purposeful future! I am not sure if it is not better to have a simple one and to avoid such pain along the way!"

"Well, that is what I have described to you just a few minutes ago. I told you, let those of lower flights fly low; and I told you, it is not necessarily better to fly very high. It just is! And if it just is, then it just is and there is nothing you can do to change that."

"Please continue, please tell me more of the signs and what they are! At least I may know them and I may save myself from excess struggles!"

"Following the sign of many previous deceits, or even a single very intense deceit, is the sign of dreams. Have you known this person in your dreams before? Who was he, or who was she? How long have you been waiting for his/her presence? How long have you been waiting to feel as you felt in your dreams at night?

But alongside this, you must be exceedingly aware and exceedingly careful! For great deceits show up in our dreams, as well! The difference is the peace. In a dream of the right one, there is a peace so still and so calm. In the dream of the deceivers, there is only desire, unbearable longing, something that is unattained, hence, the longing is unbearable and unfulfilled. Follow the peace.

And there is yet another sign! That is, if you are able to tell the person that you will leave them— even in a jesting or a casual manner— and instead you feel a deep wound forming in your heart as you listen to those words coming out of your mouth. You cannot fool around with the mere idea of leaving them— that is a very big sign! But it must be both ways, not just one way! If you feel that wound forming also in their own hearts, as you say this to them, and you feel it truly forming there, as it has formed also in your own soul, then that is one of the signs. It is a very significant one.

Lastly, I will mention the fact that there are many things that will try to stand in the way of those who have chosen to be together! There is something called 'meant to be' and there is something called 'free will'. The life of Free Will exists in the future that is already thriving, which you have chosen. There are powers that be, who would wish to plan your life for you— be it your fears, your dogma, your doubts, other people and the system around you… or perhaps those who might control the fates! Or perhaps it is more of a testing ground, an exercise ground, upon which your tenacity to stay with one another is challenged and strengthened through the overcoming of obstacles, together! OR maybe, it is actually just the process of growth— of breaking through the layers of soil, as a seed does on its way to becoming a tree."

"Can two people be 'meant to be', as well as each others' 'free will'? Can these two terms be used to describe one situation between two people?"

"Yes, it may be so. These two terms can be used to describe a single pair of individuals, or they may be used separately to describe different pairs of individuals. Some may be 'meant to be' and might not be each others' free will choice; while others make their free will choice, hence, creating their own 'meant to be' and inscribing that upon Eternal Stone!"

"How does one run away from fear? How does one get away from the plague of fear? It creeps and it crawls like a disease…"

"In your question itself, is found the reason why you are plagued by fear— in your inquiry of how to run away from it! Do you run away from a mad dog that is right beside you, or do you stand still, stare at it, anticipate its moves and overcome it? If you run from a mad dog that is inches away from you, that dog will bite you and very possibly kill you. But if you study it in those moments, anticipate its movements, you will be able to counter it and overcome it. That happened to me twice as a child, I was attacked by crazed dogs on two different instances, each only a few inches away from me. I stood still, anticipated the course of attack, and I attacked first! I grabbed onto the dog's face, each time, pulling back at the dog's skin on the side of its face as hard as I could! Each time, I sent the dog yelping and running away. Had I ran from those dogs, I would have been bitten by them! I know because I was also bitten once. I ran and climbed a tree. But dogs run faster, so that dog bit me. Luckily, I do climb fast, so it was only a surface wound. But I learned that we cannot outrun angry dogs; however, we may stand and fight and overcome them.

It is the same thing with fear. Fear need not be feared. Do you understand that? You don't need to be afraid of your fears! Your fears are only there because something else is worth it! And even if they stay there for a long time and they don't leave; that only means that many things have been, and are, worth it! Do not be frightened of fear! Anticipate its movements and counter it before it bites you! It is possible to do this. But you must remember that you are not countering the fearful circumstances in your mind that are playing in your head, that you think might be happening or that might happen soon. No, this is not about paranoia. This is in fact about countering the fear itself, the very root of what causes you to play the negative thoughts in your mind. It is not about countering the occurrence of the negative scenarios in your mind; but, it is about countering the root that causes you to think those thoughts that are very likely not happening and are not ever going to happen."

"This is a very difficult thing to do when you have dealt with deception and your worst fears actually did happen to you, before!"

"Yes, what you say is true. It is in fact a very difficult task to accomplish, especially when you have come out from a place where your worst fears *did* actually happen to you! Nevertheless, it is a necessary learning process. In this precise way— life is not easy, life is difficult in this way. We could say that life does not give us the tools that we need in order to survive, in order to surface, in order to win. And perhaps that is true. Perhaps it is not fair. Regardless, you must stand up, you must be strong, and you must overcome. And this is the way to overcome."

"How does one overcome the loop of negative relationships? It seems like we make negative relationship after negative relationship and it appears to be a nonending loop of meeting a person and thinking it is right, but then that turning sour or bitter in the end. A string of resentment, a long string of resentment, frustration and rejection— this string goes around in a circle, how do we stop this?"

"This string forms and this circle is created, when we fail to tie knots, when we fall short of making closure. People think that it is possible to simply walk away from a relationship or a friendship, without understanding the other person and without understanding themselves; without understanding why the energy changed, why their structure is bent, is crumbling… people are not designed to withstand simply being left! Do you understand what that means? Think about my words seriously— human beings are not designed to withstand simply being left. A human being must understand, a human being must understand every small detail and there must be acceptance along with that understanding. A human being must come to terms, otherwise, there will be rifts and tears in the Soul, in the Mind, in the Heart; those rifts and those tears will open up into further wounded territory, leading to more rifts and more tears… it is very painful territory we are speaking of now, and I'm sure you can feel that in your heart as I explain this to you.

In every circumstance within a relationship or a friendship, you must overcome your ego during times of misunderstandings and conflict; during times of coldness and distance, and you must do that to your ego, so that you may reach out to the person you are embattled with, to seek an understanding. Because you must reach an understanding, you must strive to understand every detail, no matter how difficult it may be for you to reach out to the other! This may result in reconciliation, or it may not result in reconciliation; but what it will *always* create, is closure! Closure is the act of tying the knot, which can only be accomplished by surpassing the ego in order to reach out to the person you think is most wrong at the moment, the person whom you might even hate so much at the moment— so that you may tie that knot and free yourself of the painful loop that plagues so many! Tie the ends, so that you may start out with a new string, having a new beginning and a new continuation. Be humble enough, because that humility will take you very far, further than those who wrong you. And it could even save a relationship you thought couldn't be saved anymore.

During this time, though, it is important and very valuable to remember that humility is not the absence of self worth. In fact, it is quite the opposite. Humility will cause you to glow and to shine, far brighter than those who would wish your downfall. To be humble does not mean to forsake your sense of self worth or even your sense of self esteem. But humility is a tool that you must use to set your future free from the dreaded loops that bind, from the restrictions that would enslave you. And why do I even use the word 'humility' in the first place? I use this word because it takes humility to stop in the moment of your rage and to accept that you may be wrong, or that, even if you are right, you will still need to reach out in order to set your future free of those dreaded things that bind. In those moments of rage, resentment and rejection, it will be exceedingly difficult to extend your hand and say, 'help me to understand you, help me to understand this', to the very person that you do not want to understand! Alas, it is ever so necessary, it is exactly what you must do. If you do this, you *will* be set free. And so you see, Freedom does not come at a low price; on the contrary, the price of Freedom is priceless. The cost of Freedom is an act that cannot be paid with money."

"What is the worst thing about living in this world? What is the worst thing about the system in this world, and the worst thing about trying to live this life?"

"The worst thing about living in this world is the fact that the main priority of people has now become to get through life with the least amount of pain possible, to get through life unscathed. To attain and to manage a happy life is already seen a luxury; while the reality is to make it through life with the least amount of wounds possible. And that is the worst thing about living here, because it has become a planet on which we are so often pained that the goal has become to avoid pain! Instead of being born into this world, and journeying on a path of joy and fulfillment, rather, we are born into this world and we journey on a path of avoiding hurt! The focus is on avoidance, on survival... this is the worst."

"How can I stop living in this worst state to live in?"

"You can stop living in that worst state to live in by identifying the fact that your fulfillment, your desires and your joys— these are all very important things to attain. The denial of happiness and pleasure in life in no way brings you closer to godliness. Naturally, there are unnatural 'desires' that are longed for by the perverted man; but, I am not speaking to the pervert nor to the dark and evil soul; I am in fact speaking to *you*! You who are pure of heart, you of holy laughter! There is no pervert who would sit with me, anyway, so for you I'm sure these words of mine will fall on fertile ears.

To you I say, that if you seek to set your joy and pleasure first, if you set it at North, and follow your compass always, then you will espace the worst thing. Do not deny yourself Peace, do not deny yourself Love, do not deny yourself Laughter, Happiness, Play! Do not deny yourself Purity! Do not deny yourself Freedom! Think of yourself as she who will never deny herself any good thing, as she who will let no one hurt her. When you do this, when you shift your view of yourself and change the way you see your direction, I promise you that you will escape the worst, and you will be happy and free. It might not happen right away, but if you stay the course, it *will* happen!"

"What about Heaven and what about Hell? How am I going to get to Heaven and how am I going to avoid going to Hell?"

"I believe that we are not determined either to

Heaven or to Hell, through our actions here on Earth. On the contrary, I believe that we come either from Heaven or from Hell, prior to this life, and we carry our prior origins inside of us, at all times. People just go back to where they originally came from. And they live in this life as a result of where they once were. Of course, we have the capacities to develop and to build and to create more, while we are here, and perhaps even to change the course of our destinies, but I believe that the soul matter of individuals are varied and are not all of the same origins.

Perhaps a human simply falls back into himself upon the disintegration of his physical body and continues to take form within the self of himself, simply returning from whence he came."

"Heaven, Hell, This World... how can we change this world, then? How can we make it into a place we can call Heaven? Or at least, how can we turn this world into a better reality?"

"You will never be able to change the world by projecting ideal images to aspire for. The only way to change the world is to penetrate the grassroots, to penetrate at the groundbreaking level— to be a mason— to dig into the core where all the tar and lumpy mud is located and to work with that shit until you bring out something beautiful. We change the world by dressing wounds, by listening to forgotten voices of the lost, by getting our hands dirty. Nobody is going to be able to change the world by painting a lovely picture. You have to know how to make paint. Then teach the people how to use a paintbrush. Then teach the people how to make strokes, how to wash the paintbrush, and how to mount their own paintings onto the wall. Because the alchemy of the world, of humanity as a whole, is really just the collective alchemy of every individual. Take what is darkness and transmutate it into a shining thing. Changing the world is never about the changer; it is about the world."

"What do you mean when you say 'grassroots'"?

"All people want to belong to some sort of hierarchy. Allow me to explain. The rich want to be the richest; the poor want to be the smartest; those who are both rich and smart want to be the better persons; the better persons want to go to Heaven;

those who are in Heaven will look down upon those who are in Hell... there is always some kind of hierarchy desired by everyone; even by those who claim the opposite of this. So how do you find true Divinity? Divinity is found in those who reach down low; because it is those who are above who must reach down low, while it is those who are below who must constantly reach for what is above! And this is Divinity. What is Divine, is what will have a curiosity in what is below. There is no fear of becoming 'tainted'; because what is lesser can never really taint what is greater. It is in fact that which is greater that is able to transform what is lesser. The Alchemist must first find the mud, pick it up, before she is able to transform it into diamond. She must first reach into the swamp, in order to pull out roses.

"What is vanity?"

"I am afraid of those who are too simple on the outside; for their vanities they wear upon their hearts. Better to meet a person who wears their vanities out in the open where you can see them! Than one who hides them in their hearts! For it is the stuff of the heart that is hidden; while the stuff on the outside is not. And we are all vain; the difference is where we put it! I would rather meet a person vain on the outside, while possessing the simplest of hearts."

"Is it truly necessary to change the world? Why do we feel like we should change it?"

"Too many people feel like they need to change the world, the nation, the city, the community... but then it usually stops there. People look out into the world, out at other people, and they want to change it, they want to change *those others over there.* Wherever you look, whatever you read, whatever you hear and you study... they are all formulas concocted by a person or a group of people who want things to be different, different according to their own beliefs. Formulas for change in order to transform others into an image more like themselves or more like what they profess to believe in.

Now, how many people are looking in towards themselves, their own families and their own souls, to scrutinize themselves and to hunt down what they should change about their own characters, about their own hearts, about their own minds? Am I

expected to listen to the one who wants to change
the whole world, when that one cannot even change
his own self, his own mind, his own heart? Is not the
world a collection of minds, hearts, and individual
selves? And so to change the world only means to
change yourself, to change the world within yourself.
In doing so, you have changed the world! And if this
is not your goal, then what is the engine of your lofty
aspirations? If that is not your trophy, then what is
the generator of your high aspirations? Would it not
only be to make others think like you do, believe like
you, do as you do, only because you believe that
what you think, believe, and do, are superior to what
others think, believe and do? There is no honour in
changing the whole population of the world to follow
as you do, to follow as you believe and as you say,
when you are simply another person trying to
persuade others. But there will always be honour in
looking into your own soul, looking at your
reflection, asking the questions, *How can I change,
How can I become better, How can I rid myself of these
flaws and these shortcomings that hurt others and that hurt
myself?* And in that same light, you must also be ready
to realise that there are some shortcomings that

cannot be adjusted and that cannot be changed; nevertheless, they are flaws, and you must know that they are flaws. You must know that flaws exist, because in our flaws are found the spaces where another one can fit, where another one may complete us. And perhaps, that other one may even show us the way and teach us how to become better versions of ourselves.

Am I supposed to subscribe to the formulas of people who cannot even hold their own hearts together? To abide by the equations of other people who cannot see what it is within themselves that is no good, that ought to be changed? I suppose you could say that I am just like them, that I am only looking to change everything and everyone around me, but nay, the only one I look to change is myself. Look at you! You are in fact me, and I am teaching you, because you *are* me!"

"What is your religion?"

"This is a funny question to ask me!"

"Yes, it is! But, what is your religion?"

"My religion is Beauty. Have you heard them all say that their religion is kindness? Well, my religion is Beauty."

"What does that mean? What does it mean when one says that her religion is Beauty?"

"When I say my religion is Beauty, I am saying that I am an advocate of the process of things becoming beautiful, becoming more; of things and of people that add joyful, pleasing, peaceful, gentle, harmless, worthwhile objects, creeds, and experiences, to their communities, and collectively to the rest of the world. I am faithful to the beautiful roses, I am faithful to the beautiful wildflowers in the fields, I am faithful to the Dawn and to the Dusk. I am faithful to the harp, to the music that it brings to my ears, I am faithful to joyous laughter and I am faithful to good and pleasing food! I am faithful to the faithful lover, to the lover who makes a house into a home; I'm faithful to the innocent child, to the child who makes a home into a sanctuary; I am faithful to the trees that give us homes to live in and bridges to cross. I am faithful to happy memories and to gentleness. I am faithful to the absence of hostility, to the absence of death. I am faithful to bliss.

I am a beliver in sublimity; in paintings and in sculptures. I am a believer in marble angels and in stone gargoyles. I am a believer in the strokes of the paintbrush that can be found nestled on the surface of oil paintings, I am a believer in the freedom of the flowers, the way that colors roam our Earth, I am a believer in form and in flow. I believe in the way the Moonlight makes me feel and I believe in the way that the Sunlight can soothe my Soul. I believe in the soft breaths that escape my lips during intimate moments, the touch of another's skin on my skin, the rubbing of another's Soul upon the membranes of my own Soul! I believe in the movement of dance and in the music that makes us want to do it. I believe in the sanctity of intimacy and in the songs that we sing. I put my faith in Myths, Legends and forgotten writings. I put my faith in the consiousness of stones and in the tales of the waters. I trust in the small animals that I feed, and in the people who understand them. I trust in metamorphosis, in growth, in the way that the seed turns into a fruit tree! I trust in my dreams at night, they are more than just dreams. I am a friend to bliss, to delight, and to those who make things beautiful and who create beautiful things. Michelangelo is my Priest. Donatello is my Saint. I worship those who can take a stone and turn that stone into a chapel.

I am the enemy of things and of people that would deceive and divide, I am enemy of corrosion and erosion, I am enemy of disease and malfunction, I am enemy of lies and of manipulations, I am the enemy of lack, of want, of need and of envy. I am the enemy of the carcass, of the rot, and of loss. I am enemy to all things that would cause ugliness and struggle in a life and in a world. I cannot be friends with those who are the cause of decay in others. Don't make me dance with someone that is envious, don't make me sit and eat with someone who stabs another in the back. This is my Creed, this is my religion.

My religion has much to do with this world in which we live, it has much to do with life in the flesh as we know it, has much to do with being alive and living. I do not look forward to death, nor do I wish it upon my loved ones. I do not hope to be neither a martyr, nor a saint. I don't want to be either of those things! I place not my hopes upon the loss of pleasure in this life, nor upon the loss of this life, itself! I adore the structures of this world and I wish to beautify them. In fact, I once became so attached to beautifying the ugly, that I found myself stuck in the ugly more than I should be, and I had to pull myself out of there in order to place myself back into Beauty.

I see nothing wrong with materialism, the same as I see nothing wrong with spirituality; I don't favour one over the other. If one man takes comfort in his possessions and the other in his meditations, who am I to judge one better than the other? In fact, we can at least see the material thing! We cannot see the immaterial thing! Would merely believing in the immaterial equate to being a better person? I think not! I am happy for those who take comfort in their corporeal possessions and I am happy for those who take comfort in their prayers. If God created both this physical world, as well as the virtue of prayer, then both the corporeal and the incorporeal are of equal value! Now, if I could only walk with one foot always in the material and the other foot always in the spiritual realm— that, to me, would be the perfect balance.

I laugh at people who do not think I am materialistic. There is no one I have ever met, who thinks I am materialistic. Everyone thinks that I detest materialism and that I am teaching separation of Body and Soul, with favour given to the Soul above the Body. This is not the case! If such were so, do you think I would look the way that I do? If I held such a belief, then my Soul would not give importance to by Body and my Body would be nothing wonderful to look upon. But such is not the case. I have *all intentions* to live this material life to the fullest and to experience what that means, to the fullest! So do not misunderstand me, do not take me for only a deep, thoughtful, beautiful soul. No, do not misunderstand me, do not take me for a brooding, contemplative, caring soul that thinks nothing of anything but what is virtuous and spiritual. Do not mistake me for a saint, a martyr, a selfless person. I may be those things, but remember that I am *equally* desirous of this world, lusting after the objects that I can touch with my hands. Poverty is not a virtue to me; selflessness is something I battle to overcome; depth is an area in the ocean that I swim in, and that I swim in very well; but I also enjoy the shoreline! I am living proof that one can be both of this world and of other worlds, equally and with matching value. Afterall, 'this world' is still 'another world', to the other worlds!

Currently, there is too much discredit of our own world, too much seeking of the worlds beyond and the worlds to come. Meanwhile, our world has many treasures to offer, many riches she wants to unfold. There are diamonds in the dirt and sapphires in the sand. There are many pleasures to be had, many joys to be felt— *here, right now, in this world.*"

"What are the religions of this world like? Those beliefs that they all adhere to?"

"The major religions of today would cause all of their followers to become martyrs: robbing them of their blood; or, saints: robbing them of their joy. And do not tell me that man finds joy in lack, because, that is an unnatural state to be in! To find joy in lack, is a result of the conditioning of the mind into emancipation. As for me, My Faith is Life! Life *is* Faith! Death is not needed to validate Faith! I will choose the paths of life, those providing me the most opportunity to live and to be joyful, and in doing this, I am practicing my own act of Faith! Life is my

Faith. *My* life is my Faith. To uphold life is to stand up for Faith and to live a beautiful life is to practice Faith.

Today, we have martyrs for vengeance and martyrs for compassion: two kinds of dead people at each end of God's two distinct arms. Why should I choose to be one of them? To fear fear itself, is the ignorance of spirituality. One is so afraid of being afraid, that he blows himself up in a bout to prove himself above fear; while the other is so afraid of being afraid, that he risks his life in foolishness, in the name of compassion (to die in the name of kindness is to die a worthy death). Why all death? Why do both of those doors lead to death? And both build their door in the name of God!"

"Why is it that the greater majority of people fall into either one of these 'hands of God'"?

"Because there is an extremism in spirituality, today. The result of spiritual extremism is the blatant disregard for the corporeal body, this physical life, and this material world; and this extremism reveals itself through the two disparate hands of God: vengeance and compassion. One will harm in the name of vengeance while the other will put himself in harm's way, in the name of compassion. Both attempt to wash away blood with blood: the one attempts to wash away the blood of his family with the family of another; while the other attempts to wash away the blood of the other with the blood of his family. But blood cannot wash away blood!

"What about you? Where does your heart lie?"

"I am a Queen, and I will always be a Queen. I will always have a heart for my own, and for my own Kingdom. My nobility dictates that I fight for my Kingdom, that I defend my Kingdom, that I ensure the continuation of my Kingdom. My own nobility dictates that I love my people, that I care for my people and that I protect my people. I am a Queen, and I will always believe in my own Kingdom; I will always love my own people; I will always love my own home; for my family I would die, to protect them I would die for them. Blood protects its own blood, family protects its own family, a love protects its own love. As a Queen, this is the nobility that I am bound to, and this will never change. I am a Queen, I always was a Queen, and I will always be a

Queen; you can never tell me that all of the people in the world are one; I am one with my love, I am one with my children, I am one with my blood and my joys and my beauties. I do have my own, and I will not squander my own, I will not let their blood flow for the blood of others— I will not. As a Queen, you will never be able to convince me that we are all one. We are not all one. We all have something of our own. We are only all one in the fact that we are all of, and to, and with our own. This is not exclusion; this is belonging! This is not seclusion; this is belonging! We all belong to our own, and those of us who know not where we belong, we search for our own until we find them.

Human beings are infatuated with virtue, believing that virtue is able to rescue them in the afterlife. So in virtue they attempt to wash blood with blood, albeit, the virtue of one is the sin of the other. Virtues are not seen as tools; rather, they are seen as idols worth sacrificing human life to. They think they have no idols, and that their Gods are unseen, living up above in Heaven, but, their idols are their virtues and upon their virtues they sacrifice human lives. It is all death and destruction, things I do not wish to have any part in.

Then there are the 'peaceful martyrs', the ones who become martyrs in this life, not thanks to others, but thanks to themselves for themselves. It is not due to compassion, not due to vengeance; but it is due to an attainment of bliss! To attain bliss, they believe, is to deny all the fives senses of pleasure, to deny the flesh continually, because they believe that bliss awaits them in a state of physical self-denial. All unnatural things! All of these martyrs are denying what is natural to the life of the human being. And the funny thing is that this is the very human thing to do! A God would know that to be also human is a gift, and would live that humanity out fully and beautifully!

What is naturally human, is naturally beautiful, and it is meant to be so. The human brain can become so easily infatuated with its own Soul, that it would seek to destroy itself in order to be entirely Soul. And what is a soul without a physical body? That is a being who cannot fulfill its destiny! What is a physical body without a soul? That is a dead body! And so body needs soul while soul needs body—

then the ignorance of man comes in and partakes of the banquet, convinced by external forces that it needs to eliminate either one of them in order to attain happiness. It is always a quest for happiness—either in the afterlife, or a physical state of bliss here on Earth. And yet, happiness has already freely been given to man, in the potential of Soul and Body! But man, stupid as he is, believes he must improvise on the works of God and take from what is already perfect. Annihilate one or the other. I don't know if I should feel pitty, or if I should be amused!

Religions claim to be the way to immortality, to Eternal Life, and yet, they teach you how to separate your physical body from your soul. The separation of Body and Soul is equivalent to death: both the death of one's destiny and the death of one's physical body. Immortality is equivalent to the unification of Soul with Body, ascending from life to Life, without death in between!"

"Is there any beauty to be found in death? What is death, what does death mean, and what really happens when you die?"

"There is indeed beauty to be found in death, yes, there is both a sorrow but then there is also a joy!"

"A joy? But how in the world can this be so?"

"After death, the soul is able to do those things which it was not able to access while abiding within the physical body. Many times, the departed loved ones are able to give back to the living, so much more than they were capable of giving while they were still abiding within their flesh and bones. It is true, in this way, that the dead become 'guardian angels'. It is true that the dead will often release their living loved ones from bondages, deceits, lies and blindness. You will often notice this— if you stop to feel and to notice it— within the first few days after the death. You will begin to see so much more than what you were before capable of seeing, you will begin to understand so much more than what you were normally capable of understanding, and you will be able to correct within yourself all those things that were leading you on a destructive path in your life. This is all the working of your departed loved one, for you.

There are so many valuable lessons that you learn, when someone close to you passes away, especially when that someone was not able to give you much while they were alive— it is usually those types who make it their first goal to give you all the good that they can give, right after they have passed on to the other side. You will begin to see the truth in others, in yourself, and in your circumstances. You will witness all the many true colours of people coming out, colours that you never saw before, they will fly out along with the circumstances that come about right after the death of someone close to them. It is in these times that you will be able to truly know the living. It is when someone dies, that you will be able to clearly see the truth about the living! And then you will also begin to see clearly the truth in yourself, the truth of your direction in life, and the general truths that everyone should hold to a high standard, such as, the reality that life really is too short to spend any amount of time on doing anything other than going into the direction of your happiness! Life is too short to hold grudges, plan vengeance, and be angry for too long. And people say things like that all the time, but words like that only take on their meaning when you experience someone close to you passing away. There are truly not enough minutes, hours, days, months, and years, to spend any amount of time on being and doing anything other than going into the direction of your happiness. Acceptance is better than correction and joy is better than revenge. Innocent laughter is better than anger.

Moreover, we learn so much about the living, by observing how the living treat their deceased friends and family. The Gods of the North have taught that even your enemy in battle, whom you have vanquished, must be treated with utmost respect at death, no less than the respect and the treatement that you would give to a deceased loved one. It is during the times of someone who has died, that we are able to build up our character, and are able to collect priceless treasures along the way, within ourselves, that we may look back upon in the future in order to say, 'Those are some of the moments, some of the instances, that I am most proud of my behaviour, of my service, of my own honour and of my own respect for others.' We see how much we value life, by observing how much we respect someone's death, and we see this in such a conclusive way, that there will be nothing to shake our newfound knowledge of ourselves. Therefore, in death, there are defining moments which sculpt us out as individuals, which will determine how we are able to see and measure our own value, in the future.

We usually believe that we must correct the faults in our loved ones and friends (and sometimes even the faults of the whole world); but death teaches us that these faults are things that are of no value and of no matter, in life and in death. The faults of others are better not seen, are better left to the Higher Powers, for the faults in others are the business of the Higher Powers, never our own business. It is better not to see the frailties and the mistakes in others, other than for the reason that we are often placed in the midst of faulty people, so that we may have the perfect example of exactly what not to be like— and that is something that we ought to be exceedingly thankful for. Having exact examples of what not to be like, is designed as a way to make our navigation more easy for us. Of course, we do not see that as the purpose of it all, when we are too busy reaching for ideals of perfection: *I wish my family members were perfect, I wish my parents loved me as much as his parents love him, I wish I was born in the country she was born in, I wish that my relatives were good and kind and lovelier than they are, I wish that I came from a happier family...* it is when we reach for our ideals of perfection, that we repeatedly throw away the opportunity to make our navigation in life easier, by simply looking at all the bad examples that we have, in order to spot precisely what we should not be like! You see, human beings are very preoccupied with emotions, feelings, and what things ought to be like; so much so, that they are so often not able to recognize the valuable gems they are given. Human beings ought to look to the Gods as an example to overcome this. The Gods are not preoccupied with feelings, with emotions, and with ideals of perfection. Gods see all the tools of benefit at hand, and put those tools of benefit to good and to perfect use. In all instances, there is a benefit. To be idealistic is to be blind to the tools immediately at hand, while to have no goals is to not have a forward-moving direction. The perfect state is the state of the Gods: To open one's eyes to the tools of benefit that are immediately at hand, while always keeping the vision in sight, no matter how faint of an image it might one day fade into; always, always keep the vision in sight, keep the goal unwavering, but then open your eyes to see the tools around you that may be used to your benefit, no matter how unideal they may appear to be! Ideals are set by pre-determined expectations, which in turn are creations of man. Gods do not always follow creations of man; Gods more often create where no man before has created!

There is yet another way that we may find beauty in death; in looking to the flowers that are offered for the deceased. Flowers that are offered for the dead do not know the difference of where their beauty will be placed, they do not say, 'This is not a palace' or 'This is not a garden'; they just are. They are just beautiful, without giving regards to whether they are placed on a grave or in a castle. Flowers are just beautiful, whether they grow by the wayside or in a manicured garden. If we were all like flowers, then we would all be beautiful, with no regards to why or how. We just are. We are just beautiful.

Lastly, it is important to remember that the word 'dead' is only our description of those who have passed on to the other side; it does not, however, mean that they are void of life! A life that we do not understand is not a life nonexistent; rather, it is a different form of life, different from our own, one that we have not yet experienced, or at least, have no memories of experiencing before.

It is extraordinary how death can give so much back to life and to the living. The dead are mourned by their family and their friends; stop to ask yourself, if you were to die today, what would your memorial look like? What would your burial look like? What would your funeral be like? Would there be many flowers overflowing— offerings from friends and loved ones? Would there be many people gathered, all come back together in remembrance of you and of long lost times? Contemplate upon what *your* death would look like, and with this newfound vision, let go of the grudges and the unforgiveness. Let go of the pride, the ego and the faultfinding— these things are of no value, both in life and in death."

"What is the 'other side' like?"

"It is far more beautiful than what we have here. On the other side, there thrive the Spirits of the Trees, Water, Air, Fire, Rocks, Mountains and

Stones… there are the things that they call 'Fae' and 'Faun'. On the other side there are the beautiful beings that we don't normally see on our side, not unless we are lucky enough to see them. The other side is continually drenched in magic, and there are no boundaries to the beauty and enticement that one can experience. The dead simply move on to the realm where living beings are not normally seen. However, I am not sure if this is the same for all. I still wonder if, perhaps, we all come from different places and we return to those different places, thus, perchance 'the other side' is different for different individuals according to where they initially came from, and perhaps, according also to what they believe in. There are many who believe in an exact 'Heaven' as described in Sacred Texts, and they believe that their souls ascend to that place as exactly described within those texts. But I wonder if those descriptions are not formulas constructed by humans, in order to make sense of things. Perhaps it is an exact science according to what one believes in, or, maybe it is not. Maybe the different descriptions are only different ways of explaining and understanding a single truth, a single place where we all come from and where we all return to!"

"But which is more likely the definite answer? Which is more likely the definite truth? I want to know what *you* believe."

"I believe that not all of us come from the same place, therefore, we are also not all returning to the same place. I believe that some of us, in this lifetime, are able to walk in and out of 'the other side', which is really just our Inner Country. Remember that Inner encompasses the Outer. By saying 'Inner', we are by no means referring to something that cannot be touched and cannot be reached, nay, when we say 'Inner', we are also describing what engulfs the Outer! Some of us walk in and out of the Corporeal and the Incorporeal, and the lines between the two become blurred as we tread over these lines again and again, in the sand. Albeit, only a very few may do this. Only a very few are hybrids born of both worlds: A Soul entirely non-human and a Body entirely Human (yet always influenced by the non-human Soul within)."

"Is there such a thing as magic? Are some people magical?"

"Yes, magic is real. And contrary to popular belief, if you are born with magic, there is no amount of disbeleif or nonbelief that will be able to remove you from the reality and the responsibility of it. It is not true that magic is only real for those who believe. Magic is an imprint on the DNA, it remains real regardless of your mental and/or emotional belief in it. And if you do not accept it, if you do not see it and embrace it, you will still have to deal with the consequences of having magic in your veins, but with no way to overcome the obstacles or to soar above the challenges. Your teachers will not be merciful; rather, they will require of you to rise up into the stature that is yours. Your enemies will not be merciful to you, either. You will have a Light that is Bright, and they will always want to snuff it out. And if you do not see your Light, if you do not Rise Up into it, this bears no effect upon the eagerness of your enemies to snuff it out. Though you lay down your life for an enemy, that enemy will still betray you. You carry a great and mighty Light, and you must know it, you must learn it, you must live it."

"What exactly *is* magic?"

"Magic is the nature of what most find to be unnatural. Magic is the nature of the few, the ignorance of many. The understanding of dreams, the visions of the future, the childlikeness of the heart, the innocence of the mind, the power of the Light (or the darkness). Magic hears and comprehends the speech of the trees, the legends of the wind, and the heartbeat of the Sun. There are many forms of magic, though all is one. It is a nature beyond this nature that is bound by gravity. This is magic."

"Explain to me the beliefs of other people, the religions of the world."

"They think that to rise above dogmatic religious teachings is to lose touch with God. But to rise above dogmatic religious teachings is to ascend closer to the heights of God. Religions are compartmentalised bits of God, gathered and formed together in different languages and different cultures, so that certain peoples may assimilate what is their own, what is easy for them to understand. Religions are particles, small areas— of God— parts that certain numbers are capable of understanding. And we see the evidence of this in the fact that a certain so and so of one religion, would condemn a certain other of a different belief. If all were standing in the likeness of God, then all would not condemn another. But since all are compartmentalised, further away from God, they do not see this; their vision is limited to accommodate only themselves and those of their own beliefs. But look at the one who has ascended beyond religious compartmentalisation— that one now flies at heights far more closer to God! Above the compartments! Up there in the air, near the skies and the stars!

Once upon a time, when I was compartmentalised into a religion, I spoke to God at all times, even walking down the corridors at school, I spoke to God and I asked God to hold my hand and put His other arm around me as I walked. And now that I transcend the compartment that I once was in, I still speak to God in the same ways, but now I hear God speaking to me in return, in many different and new ways,. God now speaks to me through avenues that I before did not know could be God-avenues! I hear the Voice in the small flowers that I notice, I hear the Voice in the lights of Dusk and of Dawn, I hear the Voice of God speaking to me through the trees, through the fauna, through the leaves and through the stones! Who knew that stones could breathe and could feel and could talk! Many stones have joy, have gladness, and feel abandoned when we forget about them!"

"Stones? Do you mean actual stones like stones from the ground and in the fields, on the pathways and on walls?"

"Yes of course, I mean actual stones. Stones that lay loose on the ground and stones that are compacted into chapel walls and steps and pathways! I mean actual stones from the Earth, yes. Why are you surprised? Is it because the stone is traditionally the symbol of a lack of feeling, a lack of emotion, a lack of Spirit and of Soul? But that tradition is not real. Stone pathways have the inscriptions of thousands upon thousands of stories written upon them! The stories of all who walked upon their way! When I walk on these pathways, myself, I am able to feel their stories as if I knew all of them, as if I lived all of them! And so, how can I be alone, wherever I am? I have the countless stories of a multitude with me, I have the inumerable whispers of those who came before me! Kings, Priests, Saints, Sinners, Lovers, Masons, Knights, Warriors, Mothers, Brothers, Sisters, Friends, Warlocks, Sages, Mages and Monks! They are all easily with me, easily found by my side!

But aside from the history inscribed upon them, which I have access to, the stones have feelings of their own. Capable of joy and of a sense of abandonment.

"How can this be so? Is this not the most absurd thing that one could ever hear?"

"No, it is not absurd. It is just so. In reality, there is so much more life than we would have ever thought possible prior to transcending the compartments of religion that we were born into. And that is why I say that when I transcended religion, I rose up to be closer to God, because, I came to know and to see a new life being breathed by many things! God is life, God is Spirit, so to experience Spirit in many different things, is to experience God in many different ways.

To lose religion is to transcend barriers. To lose religion is to stay by God's side. God did not create religion— man did. God is God. People have struggled to understand God, thus created barriers as a result. The more that you come to know God, the more that you transcend towards God, and it is the more that you will lose your religion. Your religion, in fact, will become everything that brings delight to your very Soul, because therein lies the knowledge that God is with you.

"Who is God? What is God's name? And is there only one God or are there many?"

"There is a different name for God in every religion. However, that is not very important to know. What *is* more important is to know your Father! Long before a child learns its father's name, it calls its father, *daddy!* And the father is a daddy to that child. It is the same with God. Why would it be more important to know God's name? It is more important to know that you have a Father! Is it more important to know the name of your daddy than to know that he is daddy? Of course not! It is all the same with God!"

"Are there many Gods?"

"The answer to that depends upon what you mean when you say 'God'. There is only one God to each religion. Each believing their own God is the only one. So in that case, there is only one God to the man who has only one God! But to the man who hears the voice of God from even the smallest of things, from flowers and from light and from stones— there are many Gods! There is a God of Thunder, a God of Earth, a God of Tree, a God of Stone, a Goddess of Rainbow, a Goddess of Dawn, a Goddess of Rose! You could call them all the different voices of one God, or, you could see a different God speaking each a different voice! It does not matter! It is the same thing as the infant in the arms of its mother, who hears many voices saying its name, comforting it, calling out to it, cooing at it— must the infant know which one is Almighty? Is this important for the infant to know? Nay, but the only important thing for the infant to do, is to trust that it will be loved, cared for, and protected— regardless of which one of those 'voices' is going to do all of these things for it! Is it more important for the infant to identify who these kind voices belong to, or, is it more important that those kind voices are in fact there to admire the baby and to bring gifts unto it?"

"So, there are many Gods?"

"You are stubborn, aren't you?"

"Yes, I am stubborn, not much unlike you!"

"To me, there are many Gods, yes."

"Is there one God above all Gods?"

"I suppose there is a God of all other Gods, but He is more interested in reaching and touching all living beings, than in being perceived as the One God. So if I were to experience God through the Thunder, through Thorr; or if I were to experience God through Wisdom, through Athena; then this would all be a great delight to the One God, moreso than being perceived as the One God more powerful than all the rest. And in this, we should all be glad! For if it were not this way, then what a self-absorbed and selfish God we would all have! It is the same thing as the many voices of those who speak to the small infant child— if it were important to one of those voices that the infant know only his/her voice above all the rest, then this would be a very selfish person only interested in his/her own selfish motives. But it is the joy of everyone gathered around the child, that the child is loved and cared for by all the others around, as well. And this is the only interest. It is the same with the Gods!

If there is One God above all others, then that God is the Father of all the others. Is there any good father who would seek after his own recognition above the recognition of his sons and daughters? A good father does not think of himself; rather, a good father desires to see his children rise and shine, even brighter than himself! If such good fathers can be found among the humans, do you not think that the human father is better than the Heavenly Father? The Father of all Gods, the God above all Gods, is not angry and is not jealous of His own.

Frankly, I do not understand why there wouldn't be many Gods. There are many races of people, there are many types of flowers, there are many varied bodies of water… there are many different kinds of everything! So why would there only be one God? Is humanity not a reflection of God? Is the Earth not a mirror of the God Nature? If so, then there cannot be only one God, because there are many different living and natural beings and objects. Is there ever only one story? No, every person has their own story, then every land has their own story, then every culture has their own story… there are probably many different stories of many different Gods… why cannot they all be real as all the many different types of flowers are real, as all the different types of people are real, as all the different depths of water are real?"

"What is the best kind of man to find?"

"What a strange question to suddenly ask."

"I think no question is strange, don't you agree?"

"This question is strange. But I didn't say that strange has something wrong with it, did I?"
"Then do tell me! What is the best kind of man to find?"

"This is actually a very good thing to ask, because it is simple, and the answer is simple. And of course, many women should be asking this simple question instead of the other many questions they ask pertaining to men. The best kind of man to find is the kind of man who knows how to find the signs. And this is a very crucial thing, because if you are to know a man who cannot understand any sign, nevermind how loud it is broadcast into his face, that is the time you should know that you know a man whom you would be better off not knowing.

I used to know a man who did not understand anything that was shown to him by God, by the world, by the universe, by angels, or by me! I once asked him to send me some pebbles from a Croatian beach he was camping on, because the pebbles on their beaches look magical, you see. He ignored my request and then the next day, he told me all about how a small baby who could barely walk, wobbled over to him to hand him a pebble she'd picked up on the seashore. He said it was the most heartwarming thing. Of course, he didn't understand the connection between my request which he had ignored and what had happened the very next day with that baby. But that is only one small example out of probably a thousand ways he did not see things. Some people can see a thousand things in a thousand ways, while others look at a thousand things and see zero of them! Such people are not meant for you. They are meant for someone else, who will perhaps be able to also see the zero that they see. And they ought to be very happy together!

And then there is a man I know now, who is able to see the signs in all things that he looks at. Signs from God, the world, the universe, and me! He reads all the unseen scripts that are engraved into everything, he deciphers these, he understands these, and then he applies these to his life. And then, he is not afraid to apply the codes that he cracks, to the ways he sees and understands and communicates with me. He is humble. People who are able to receive messages from mundane places and understand and revere those same messages, are humble people. If the Gods were to give a profound, golden message to a crow, perched upon the crow's tongue inscribed in Elysian Gold, the arrogant man would never be able to receive this message, because the arrogant man would just shoo the crow away! It is the humble man who would take the time to notice anything different, in the first place… *why are there golden fingerprints on this crow, why is this crow bringing something to me in its mouth, why do I sense that this something is important and meant just for me?* Only a humble man would even consider listening to a crow!

It is a paradox that the most magical of things may be found in the most mundane of places. Aprhodite was born of sea foam. Diamonds come from inside the Earth. Runes are inscribed in the simplest of places, yet are some of the most powerful of symbols. If there were to come a goddess into a man's life, born of a seashell, only a man of pure heart could see her as Goddess; because, the stupid man would be looking for goddess in Temple and in Palace! The stupid man would not see the Goddess arisen from a seashell."

"You've mentioned the word Goddess… when I think of 'Goddess', the first thought that comes to mind is Venus. Can you tell me more about what She is like? So that I may understand her and so that I may understand her teachings."

"Because people have a weak understanding of the natural attributes of the Goddess Venus, they have misinterpreted her role in the Pantheon, but this misinterpretation is purely a result of a lack of understanding into the nature of the attributes. Sex is sacred, Love is sacred, Beauty Unfading is sacred. These three, in their full forms, are emanations ascribed to the Goddess, emanations which are so high, that they are seldom fully reachable in understanding by human beings. Venus is therefore the Goddess of the Sacred, the Guardian of the High Forms, Vanguard to the Wonders of Existence. They think that sex is something easily come by and easily lost, something exchanged for mere wanton pleasures and disposable fun; so they paint an image of Her as one who disregards The Act as something meaningless. But The Act is never meaningless to Venus— not the pleasures derived from it, not the warmth that comes from it, and not the bond that it was created for. The Act is a door between two souls, two bodies, and two worlds; a Sacred Door that is holy in and of itself. They think that love is unreal, because they see love as something only fulfilled in perfection. But Venus knows that Love is in fact fulfilled in *imperfection*, that Love is fulfilled not through correction, but through acceptance; not through judgment of what is weaker and deemed lesser, but through the embracing of *what is*. Love is valiant, Love is brave, and Love is true. They think that beauty is shallow, skin-deep and only something fleeting, a candy for the eyes. But they know not what Venus knows— that Beauty requires insight into even the minutest details of life and of living things and of those inanimate objects that the living do create. With no insight, with no pure vision into *what is,* without the insight into all things the way that they mundanely are, no one will be able to experience Beauty and to thrive in it. Beauty is not skin-deep; Beauty is of the depths of the deepest oceans, and continually renewing, like the fastest-flowing rivers. Beauty must dig deep, must swim deep, and must see more and fly higher, in order to create and to bring forth that essence of Herself which is buried in the simple. Beauty that is only skin-deep should not be called Beauty, at all! It should be called something else... I don't know what, but, it shouldn't be called Beauty!

So as you can see, people misrepresent Venus, because they have a tremendous lack of understanding of Her attributes. And that is all the more reason that they need Her!"

"And what about woman? What is the best kind of woman that a man can find?"

"It is the same answer for woman! It is still the woman who understands the signs that are shown to her. And not the one who thinks that everything is a sign even if it is not— but the one who knows when inscriptiosn are written by the Divine Fingers onto the walls! Just like the best kind of man to find, the best kind of woman to find is the one who is aware of her surroundings on the outside of her body, as well as the surroundings on the inside of her Soul. Simply put, the best kind of person you can find, is a person who can read and write and talk! But read and write and talk not in human terms; but, read and write and talk in terms of the Divine. But remember, so much of the Divine is first discovered in the place of original simplicity! Divinity is revealed to the pure of heart."

"What is the best kind of person?"

"How do you love the ones whom you love? How much love are you capable of knowing, having, giving? Because this is the measure of your person, this is the measure of your success, this is the measure of the highest capacity of your mind and your soul— the measure of the entirety of you. Do you love deeply and widely? Do you love fully and truly? Ask yourself these questions, because without the answers to these questions, there is nothing about you, there is no you, you are something very forgettable.

Always remember that the most valuable thing that you can do in this world, is to live a life of love. Love truly those who were given to you to be loved. Love truly the gifts you were given in life, as well as your ability to live and share those gifts. Even if the only people who remember your name are the five people you have loved and who have loved you in this life, that makes you no less important than the person who is recognised by every individual in this world! In seeking to change the world out there that you live in, do make sure that you are not changing it in order to make it become more like you; rather, live to change yourself, to know yourself, to grow and to become. This is the highest reach of man. The downfall of world-changers in this day and age, is that those who wish to change the world, only wish to influence the world of their own beliefs, choices, and opinions. But this is not how the world is changed. This planet is changed only when we heal and grow and know the worlds within ourselves. Because it is in the healing of worlds unique and innumerable that this one we share will find her hope. The only person who needs to know you, is you. And then the people who are given to you to love, who love you truly in return."

"I think you are saying, that the best kind of person to be, is the kind of person who knows, grows, becomes… the kind of person who is not preoccupied with influencing the world; rather, who knows that there is a world within, and who knows that the most important thing is to know herself or himself, and to be known truly and loved truly, by the few whom she or he truly loves."

"Yes. But it is even simpler than that. I am saying that the best kind of person, is the person who knows how to love deeply and truly."

"What about sex? Is sex at all important? Love is very important, so sex must not be as important as we think it is…"

"Sex is the most pleasurable experience that the human being can have. Believe me, I do not think it is of lesser importance in this life. I am both fully spiritual and fully carnal. Of course, there are various forms of love, and naturally, sex does not go hand in hand with all forms of love. But when comparing sex with the love that does naturally lead to sex, remember that sexual attraction is carnal and desirable, while Love is rarer and more desirable. There are those who have sex with different people every other day, but they do not Love them, and in their lives they desire Love because they do not have it. Sex does not lead to lasting relationships, lasting connections, fulfillment and the building of a life story. Love leads to all of that. However, the human mind has been misled and conditioned into believing that we love one type of person and we lust another type of person; this need not be the case! My respect for my own Lust is so high, that I would not dare Lust someone whom I could not Love. My Lust is not worth trash; but my Lust is of high value, of high worth. I Lust whom I wish to Love. And may the one whom I Love, be the one whom I so Lust. Love is worth waiting for, yes, but so is Lust. My Lust is also of high value, it is also worth waiting for!"

"What are the most beautiful qualities that a woman can have? And do you think that we are not seeing beauty of the woman in her true light or to her full extent?"

"Peaceful, serene women of great capability to think and to feel, are so often overlooked in this world in favour of the loud and the ambitious. There is nothing wrong with ambition, but when I say 'ambitious', I mean those who place an agenda into everything that they do and say. And it is difficult for young girls of serene nature to still feel like they are seen and valued, in a world where there are so many other girls who push and who shove in order to receive attention. So often, the gentle heart is not seen, it seems, and the men give their time to the loud ones, the ones to clamour for their attention and flatter them endlessly. It's hard for young girls of stillness, when they feel like they are overpowered by noisiness and constant movement. And when I say 'stillness', I mean the gentleness of the heart. When I say 'constant movement', I mean the distraction of the mind to always chase after a thing, an object, an ideal.

There are still girls who are born with a vision of themselves, and of the world, who are born with a calmness, a contentment. Hatred and vexation are far from their hearts. But then, too much of the time, they become overlooked and forgotten while they are in their natural state, and sometimes, what is theirs is taken away from them. The natural state of these girls is often forsaken and replaced with defenses and a sense of betrayal. They learn to clamour and to fight, they force themselves to hustle and to wrestle with the odds that they feel are stacked against them, that they feel have made life betray them.

But then later on, humankind grows up, humankind matures, and then they see that they have been long deceived by the noise, by the greed, by the insecurities; they leave all of that behind in search of the serene and the sincere! They mature into the knowledge of the truth, that truth being that serenity and gentleness are things more valuable that what any money can buy, and in fact, if they could pay all of their money for these, they would, because these measure up to more worth than all of the money that they have!

In other words, some girls are born into a world at the height of Beauty, which their generation only later matures into with the eyes to see and the mind to comprehend. They are Goddesses born to humans; humans who are yet to evolve to the state of comprehension of their Beauty. A Goddess does not fight to be the most beautiful one; because a Goddess knows her Beauty is rivaled by none! And yet, many Goddesses fall, for they are not seen. Many Goddesses lose their beautiful wings, for they are not sought after. Humans have many times stolen the gifts of the Gods, leaving the Gods in want, with tears that flow and drip to the ground!

The most beautiful traits for a woman to possess, are stillness, serenity, gentleness of heart. At first, perhaps a storm will call your attention, maybe the loud winds will capture your imagination; but I tell you that it is the quiet lake which you will truly long for. It is the softly bubbling brook that will become unforgettable.

There is a Beauty in woman so Divine, when she is able to drink of the softness of her own heart, of the stillness of her own inner lakes. This is a Beauty that will flow through her skin and soak through her hair. It will spill forth through her eyes. She is the golden chalice from which these serene waters of Beauty may be had.

Yes, they would reduce the Goddess to naught if they could get away with it. And yes, many have before been reduced to naught. And yes, there are those Goddesses who will rise and reclaim what is their own, never to be deceived and robbed, ever again!"

"What is it like to be a beautiful woman?"

"It is difficult to be a beautiful woman, contrary to popular belief. A beautiful woman must prove that she is more than beautiful; whereas, a plain woman must simply show that she is in fact beautiful. For a plain woman, it is a great feat to say, 'I am beautiful just the way that I am', thereby she becomes a hero in this world. But for a beautiful woman to become a hero in this world, she must become so much more than what she was born as. She cannot simply say, 'I am beautiful just the way I am', unless she wants to be stoned by the masses. A beautiful woman is not allowed to know or to see that she is beautiful; but the woman that is unattractive is allowed to see and to know that she may be beautiful if she only believes it to be so. And so, we have another type of hypocrisy in that, it is those very same people that attribute vanity as the worst thing on Earth, who dictate that it is a great, heroic act to believe oneself to be beautiful, and yet, crucify the one who was born truly beautiful if she but show a hint of awareness of her own beauty! These same people preach that it's not what's on the outside that matters, but it is what's on the inside that counts. Therefore, they are hypocrites. If it is indeed what is on the inside that counts, then don't bother trying to take from others what is their own. If it is in fact what is on the inside that counts, then don't try to detract from the happiness of others and what is their own. If it is indeed what is on the inside that matters, then focus on what is on your own inside, because that is the nearest 'inside' that you are ever going to get close to! If it is indeed the stuff of the inside that matters most, then there should be no reason to care if a beautiful woman knows that she is beautiful—because that would be just an insignificant thing, should it not?

And so, Beauty is a great and weighty thing to bear. Once you have it, you will bear the weight of it throughout a lifetime. There is always more weight that comes along with Beauty, and there is a struggle on the inside to learn how to dance with that weight and to still dance gracefully. In our societies, we see many beautiful women crumble under that weight—those who have not learned to dance with it gracefully. And then after they fall, they are crucified down low, onto crosses painted onto the ground, painted there by those who once gazed upon them before they were fallen, wishing that those they gazed upon would one day fall!

Beauty of a woman is like a superpower, in that, it can go either incredibly great or incredibly wrong for the one who bears it. If she learns to balance the weight, and to balance it gracefully, then her Beauty may very well take her to higher hieghts! But if she crumbles under its weight, she will be crucified to the ground. This is similar to a 'mutant' who knows how to harness her powers, compared to the other 'mutant' who does not. One will rise, and one will be nailed to a post."

"Then tell me, what is the correct way to see Beauty? Because it seems like it is seen in a way that it shouldn't be seen, and that is why all these people have no knowledge of handling the Beauty in others that they behold, or in themselves that they possess!"

"Beauty must be seen correctly, in the way that it was meant to be seen. First, you must know how to correctly spot it. A true Beauty is a Beauty undefiled, it is pure, unadulterated. It does not struggle to be— it just is. It gives you both peace and awe. Secondly, you must know its worth! It is worthy to be recognized, it is worthy to be appreciated, and it is worthy to be desired and kept. If you are beautiful, you must know you are beautiful, and you should say that you are beautiful, and you should feel free to say that you are beautiful! Just like the way the unattractive woman is free to think and to say such things, about herself. Beauty should be acknolwedged where it is and as it is. There is no need to deny its existence where it may be found and there is no need to find it where it cannot be found! It is not a word that must be applied to all things! Just the way the word 'ugly' may not be applied to all things; beauty must also not be seen as something applicable to all things! Many things are unsightly, many things in this world cannot be called beautiful. Just as red is not green and green is not blue, we must see Beauty where it is and how it is, without feeling the need to filter it through our own explanations and our own haggling!

Beauty is the highest state to attain. It is not something lowly. Yes, it may be found in the simplest of all places on Earth, but no, that does not mean that it is of low nature. Simplicity is not lowliness. Simplicity is grandeur; simplicity is totality; simplicity is, in fact, the evidence that something is so complete in itself, that it has allowed itself to be found evident and abundant, even in the most mundane of places."

"What about elegance? We often hear about how important it is for a woman to be elegant. And did you not hear your own parents discussing this between themselves, that they planned to raise you to become an elegant woman? Do you remember that conversation they had, long ago, when you were just a small child?"

"Yes, I do remember that conversation. In fact, when I think of what my parents would be happy to see me as, I think of elegance. They would be happy to see me elegant. And I do believe that elegance is an important thing for a woman to have, but I also know that when many women say the word 'elegant', they don't actually know what they are talking about. They say 'class', 'classy' and 'elegant', but when they say these words, they are thinking about a manner of dressing or a manner of talking or a brand name of clothing or designer handbags... they don't know that to cultivate elegance, means to cultivate a glowing inner peace; they don't know that to cultivate class means to cultivate the refusal to react to impulses of vengeance and anger. Having a fuse that is easily lit by antagonism and by harshness is the opposite of class. Anticipating the worst treatment from another person is the opposite of class. Being able to cover a multitude of sin in another, while realising that acceptance is better than correction— that is class. Knowing that we are not judges of others— that is class. Keeping the best of ourselves for those closest to our hearts— that is class. Living in the moment, respecting the feelings of others— this is sophistication. Elegance, class and sophistication, are indeed important traits for a person to have, but only when they understand how to truly cultivate those things within themselves."

"How exactly are these important traits cultivated within ourselves?"

"Simply through the denial of our basic urges. Basic urges are unpolished and unattractive— deny those— resist laziness, resist disrespect, resist judgmentalism, resist the feeling of always being shorthanded and rejected, resist the urge for vengeance, resist the blame game. Resist the primitive urges of flesh, overcome those with Elegance of Mind, and you will have begun the great work of cultivation of these certain aspects of Beauty."

"Elegance of Mind? What is Elegance of Mind?"

"Elegance of Mind is the serenity of thought, the absence of struggle within the thoughts, the absence of second-guessing and paranoia. This is Elegance of

Mind, and this translates to an elegant attitude and an elegant, graceful movement of the body. Know you not that the pattern of the mind becomes visible in the physical body? Oh but it does!"

"This is not the first time that you have mentioned vengeance. Do you mean to say that we should not seek justice, and that justice is not real and should not be desired?"

"Never would I mean such a thing. Justice is something difficult to come by in this life, and yet, we must yearn for it and hold onto it; we must pray to have it! Justice must be always on our side if we are to sail above the waters of this life.

There is a great injustice in this world, and that is, that we have no control over the circumstances and the situations we are placed when we are born into this world. Yes, there is of course the angle that we choose where we are born and how we are born, for reasons that we soon forget about, but even that angle would not alter the fact that we are greatly affected by the circumstances that we are born into. Some of us are born into difficult family scenarios, where there is little to no affection! Many people are simply born, fed, and then forgotten about; or

worse, even maltreated and abused! Circumstances
such as those take a great toll on those people. But
that is not even the great injustice that I am referring
to; the great injustice that I am referring to is the fact
that, *regardless of the places that we come from, we are still
entirely responsible for the places that we are going to and
for the choices that we make.* If you have come from a
difficult place, this does not entitle you to be difficult
to others, it does not entitle you to hurt others. And
yet, many are born and grow in beautiful places
(metaphorically and literally); but their responsibility
is not greater than yours— it is only the same! If you
have climbed from the bottom of the mountain, up
unto its peak, wind-bitten and wounded and all, in
order to stand at the peak and reach to touch the
clouds, this does not make you better than the person
who was born on top of that mountain's peak, who
simply reaches out to touch the clouds from birth
until death! It doesn't make you better, and it
doesn't even give you an excuse to become anything
less than what the one born on top of the mountain
peak has become!

This is a great injustice in life, in that, though
your path may have been harder, darker and rougher,

you must still strive to become a shining light, a beacon of joy, a cause for beautiful laughter. Your past will never be a rightful excuse for what you make of your future, *because you are not your past*; you are in fact your future. And so as you can see, the great injustice has become a great justice, in the light that you will never be held down unto what you once were and what you once had; rather, you will always be held up to the standards of what you can still become and what you can still have. In the initial injustice is found the final justice.

Justice is something we must strive for and towards, not only to become the embodiment of the final justice; but to be seen through eyes of justice in others. The latter can be achieved through prayer, and it is not in question which God you believe in, or if you believe in any God at all; because 'prayer' is something that anybody can do, and anybody can be heard for. To seek the help of anything that may be above you, so that the eyes of justice in this world will be always on your side— this is an act of prayer. Justice is so important, that we must not wait for anything bad to happen in order to seek for vengeance afterwards; but instead, we must seek justice to always be on our side, to be the voice that cries out into the night, 'This soul may not be touched by calamity, this body may not be ravaged by destruction, this heart will not be broken!'

To seek vengeance is to seek a reaction to a misfortune, to a misdeed. When you have a mind for vengeance and a heart that is turned towards it, you are nourishing a mind and a heart towards reactions to negative occurrences in your life— stop that. Stop it! Do not prepare yourself for the overflow of the worst; rather, prepare yourself to be on the favourable side of justice, at all times, which will keep you far away from the worst!"

"What then, is your general message? Are you saying that we must always give of ourselves, that we must always give and give and give? Are you saying that we must live a life of self-denial and become advocates of all-around selflessness?"

"Never would I teach such a thing. I have a golden box filled with very fine chocolate bars, and I believe that those whom I share my chocolate bars with is entirely up to my own discretion. We are all born with a golden box filled with fine chocolate bars, and the outcome of our day-to-day lives is influenced greatly by the choices we make with our chocolates! I used to believe that all people deserved my chocolate bars, and so I gifted everyone with these! Everyone who came along! Time and time again, I learned through heartache after heartache, that my chocolates were not meant to be given out to just anybody. I was taught to always share, to always make what was mine into everyone else's. I was taught 'co-ownership' of my chocolates! It is after much heartache that I learned, that I must rise up into my highest stature wihout bending down to gift everyone with my chocolates! That is a right which we all have and hold, and I tell you, that those who handle their chocolate bars wisely throughout their lives, are those who have the most chocolate bars left in their golden boxes! It is a very simple principle. The more that you give away your chocolates, the less chocolates you are going to have!

I am never saying that to have an Elegance of Mind you must sacrifice yourself continually. It is not a sacrifice of yourself that I am telling you about; rather, it is a rising up into your elevated nature that I am showing to you; then it is always up to your own discretion to choose who is worthy of your chocolates. And we do not determine another person's worth based upon their flaws or absence of flaws; rather, we determine another person's value in our lives based upon their capability to be grateful, to be thankful. What is the point in giving a good gift to a person who does not know how to identify the value of it? What is the point in giving a diamond to those who do not know the worth of a diamond? What is the point in giving a fine chocolate bar to the one who knows not the difference between fine chocolate and a raw cacao bean? There is no point, and I promise you, that if and when you do try to teach others the worth and the value of these, you will never be able to. The quality of identifying and appreciating worth is not a taught trait— it is in fact inborn. There is never any use in giving a gift to someone who does not know the worth of it. And this is how we determine the worth of another person— by their ability to see the worth in your gifts, in yourself, and in others. Are they grateful people, are they thankful people? If not, then do not even bother with them.

Give your fine chocolates away with much discretion, do it very wisely. As for me, I reserve the right to choose who may have a taste of my chocolate, for I know that in doing this, I will also reserve for myself Serenity of Mind."

"I have so many storms in my mind, and a rage that often calls to me… how can someone like me gain Serenity of Mind, and gain Elegance of Mind? How can someone with a stormy mind like mine override the typhoons and the cyclones? There are sea monsters and they entice me into their lairs… Oh please, please write a letter to me, one that I may return to over and over again, every time the winds pick up and the storms begin to rage and the waves begin to crash and to flood! Write a letter to me with words so soothing that the poison of the mermaids will be pulled from my veins and become no more! Oh please, please write me a letter and I will turn it into a song and I will sing this song whenever the lightning strikes and the hurricanes roar!"

"Dear one, you sound so troubled, you sound needful and afraid… of course I will write you this letter you ask of me, with my whole heart I will.

Here is my letter for you, read it again and again when you feel your mind slipping from the place of elegance, read it again when you feel the doubts and the rage kick in, unfold this paper again and again, until it is old and worn.

If you're reading this, that means another storm is starting up. The waves are starting up. The waves are starting to rise with the winds. Read this because you can stop the storm. Read this because you can control it. Read this because you are in control of those winds and those waves. It feels tempting, almost beautiful, but trust me, if you do not hum the song of peacefulness, those waves will destroy the houses that you've built, those winds will knock down the castles that you've built, as they have so many times before! As the storm builds, it feels like it's the first time, but that's just the lie of the mermaids! You've been there before, it has wrecked relationships before, it has blinded you before— don't listen to the mermaids! They lie; they make the lure of the oceans sound so sweet, but if you let the storm rage within you again, like you have a hundred times before, you will find yourself broken again, as you have found yourself broken a hundred times before! You will find yourself in pieces on the seashore along with the debris of the waters, along with shells, sea glass, and broken whiskey bottles.

Because the storm will break the goodness that you have built! The fear will tear you away from your magic! And it's hard, I know it's hard, because they have been so mean to you, so cruel to you, it's easier to believe that they are all like that, it's easier to believe that they are all liars and thieves, bandits and whores! But trust me, please, please, please trust me! Trust me when I say that you are too great a spirit to fall to these thoughts, to this storm, you have come so far and you have come too high, so much will be lost if you fall now, so much will be lost if you give in now! So don't. Please don't. Until one day, the song of the mermaids won't even sound beautiful to your ears anymore. It won't even sound true, anymore! Until the day that you realize the song is a lie and that the fear and pain is a lie. You were never actually hurt, because nothing can hurt you unless you believe in the pain. Until the day when their song loses its appeal— don't listen to the mermaids!

Are you ready to step so far away from the hurts, the fears and the pains, so far that you no longer even believe that they exist? Because it is time for that now. It is time to do it. Now. Not later.

Now. The storms have destroyed too many relationships, too much time, they've dragged you down for too long, the mermaids have dragged you down for too long with their lying song! The fear, the remembrance of the pains, the doubts, the wonderings— they have all morphed into these storms that bring you so much anguish! The mermaids call them in from afar; mix them with the winds, to imprison you! Nevertheless, you are the Goddess of the Seas, you are the Goddess of the Oceans, the Winds, the Skies! Roll your eyes at the mermaids. Be of sound mind. Control the tides, control everything! Do not give in to the storm; there is no good that comes from it!

If you give in again, there will be a disruption in the process of unveiling your will, your magic and your desires. It is a trick. Trust me, believe me, because I know. Because I am you. It puts you at the risk of losing the beautiful things that you are building. Don't put yourself there."

"What kind of mermaids are there? I want to know so when I see them, I will know what not to listen to."

"There is the mermaid that cloaks your eyes with lies spun from the envy of others. She is made from the envy from people's eyes and she pulls veils over the eyes of those who are envied, so that they may not see who they are, so that they may not see what they are, so that they will look around them and only see the weights and the chains placed upon them by the envious that stand and gaze! This mermaid calls to the mists and to the fog of the waters of the early morning and sings the song to cast these vapors in front of your eyes, so that when you look at yourself in the mirror, or when you look at yourself in the heart, you will see what the children of the mud want you to see, so that they may pleasure in your lack of sight, so that they may pleasure in your blindness, in your unawareness of the many things about you that are enviable. The children of the mud will dance around a bonfire, they will celebrate, as you waste your Beauty on seeking to please those who do not approve of you! But they do not actually disapprove of you; they are envious of you! This is the mermaid of the vapors of blindness, the mermaid of the morning fog!

In your life, you have found yourself continually pulled down by a wrong vision of yourself, you have not seen your own beauty because they told you it was naught. They told you that you were strange, you were weird. They told you that you were meant for servitude, that you were meant to serve this race, to bow down and to be 'humble'. But this is a lie, it was always a lie, you were not born for servitude, you were not born for this race; you were born for yourself and to find your own path. You are not meant to be infatuated with this race of people. You have taken up the cup of service, you have been given a name called selflessness, you have been taught to turn your face away from your own Beauty…taught to see yourself as nothing of greatness. But who is teaching you these things? Is it not those who are lesser than you? Is it not those who are not beautiful like you are Beautiful? Is it not those who cannot do what you are capable of doing? Who is teaching you these things? Is it not those who are ignorant? Is it not those who are born in the small corners of this Earth? Born in holes in small cities? And you allow them to teach you? And you allow them to blindfold you? And you allow them to try and take away the gifts that are your own? You allow them because you love them! You allow them because you hope in the beauty that you perceive inside of them (it is not actually there). You allow them because you think they are beautiful when they are in fact not!

You allow the mermaid to blind you with her song of vapors and fog. Why do you do this? Why don't you look into the mirror and see who you are? Why don't you look into the mirror and remember where you are from! You are not born of holes in the Earth! You are not born of mud and of dirt! The mermaids pay homage to you and bow down to you, *when you know who you are!*

You have begged people to love you, as if they cannot see your worth! You have begged them, because you yourself cannot see your worth! You have begged people to love you, creatures who would be lucky to even know you! You have begged people to love you, creatures who profit off your presence in their lives! You have come down to Earth and begged for a fallen race to love you— you who are not fallen, you who are not lost! It is not you who needs them, it is in fact they who need you!

There is another mermaid who lies to you, she tells you that you were born for service, she tells you that you are only worth what other people make of your service; as a result, you do things for people in exchange for approval! You give things to people, hoping for their approval! It is a song that she sings, a song of forgetfulness and you begin to forget your birthright, your entrance into this world, you begin to forget who you are and why you came here, you start to think that you are your religion! You start to think that you are the songs that you sing in church, you start to think that you are who your mother wanted you to be. You think that you need to fix everything; you think that you need to have patience with everyone; you need to heal the land and the people! You stretch your body over the lands as a living sacrifice and you cry out, 'God, use me as your lamb upon the rock!' Time and time again I have watched you sell your soul when all you should be doing is filling your own soul with love and with gentleness! Fill your soul with the wine of life!

You were not born a warrior for mankind; you were born to walk in gardens! You were not born a hero of the people; you were born to walk in gardens! You were not born to lay down your life for the sick, for the needy, for the world! You were born to walk in gardens! You were born here to find emeralds and rubies! Forget the name that they gave you, that name of the servant! You were born to chew on sapphires and diamonds! You were born to be lavished with aquamarine and larimar! You are Goddess of the mermaids, *when you look into the mirror and see who you are!*

There is yet another mermaid who wants you only for her own, she lies to you and sings the song that they are all the same. She lies to you and sings the song to you of unforgiveness and pain. She calls to you over the rocks of the seas and she says that all will end the same, that he will be like the other one, who was like the other one, who was like the other one and the other one… but the fact is that they were all never the same and they will never be the same! You heard her song and began to sing it, you heard her song and began to sing it to the men, and in their eyes, you became someone of stupidity and fear! And in their eyes you became a woman of stupidity and lack. It is a song that is not your own, it is a song that is sung by the abandoned and the weak; you are not abandoned and you are not weak! It is a song that is not your own; it is a song that was sung by your mother and her friends, by the creatures around you and their friends, by the magazines and their stories! It is not your song!"

"What is my song?"

"Your song is a song like a lighthouse in the darkest of nights, your song is a song that is sung by bright and shining things! Your song is one of transformation, a song that turns rocks into diamonds! This song of yours is one that she (the mermaid) has wanted you to forget, because with your song, you do not need her! Because with your song, you do not need the fear to make you feel safe! With your own song that is brave, that is holy, you do not need her lies to tell you that she will protect you from everyone! You don't need to keep on pushing people away!"

"What does my song sound like?"

"Your song sounds like the voices of the birds that visit you in the morning. It sounds like the chants of the monks in Spain. Your song sounds like one of purity and strength, of freedom and desire, of victory and immortality! You sing the song that only the dead can sing because they have overcome life by ultimately leaving this Earth; but you do not need death to overcome life! Your life is an act of victory! *This* is your song! So listen to me, please, listen to me when I say that it is time to remember who you are and what you have, it is time to renounce the pain that was never yours to begin with! Those are the pains of others around you, not your own! You are not victim to anyone, you never were and you never will be! So do not sing her victim song, do not sing her song of loss and of weakness. Take up your own song of the Gods, Demi Gods and Angels! You are Goddess of these mermaids, *when you remember your song!*"

"Thank you for this letter, I will read it and read it again and then again... if only I can remember to do so, whenever the feelings of rejection kick in, whenever the thoughts of worthlessness creep around, whenever the fears and the unforgiveness are near. But I would also like to ask you, if you are in fact telling me that I should not give to the needy, should not share with those who lack… should I not help a friend in need, or care about the people who need care and also care for this world that we live in? For this planet that we live in? Should I go about self-centered and selfish, only thinking of my desires and my purpose? What about the desires and the purposes of the others? So I must clarify, is this what you mean?"

"Of course not. To be on this Earth for the purpose of servitude is entirely different from to give and to share and to care from the goodness of your own heart! Do you think that a servant serves out of love? Perhaps in an ideal utopian society, this would be so! But how many servants in this world do you think would like to remain as servants, giving to their masters all that is required of them to give? To see yourself in a position of service always, is not at all the same thing as seeing yourself in the position of caring, sharing, and being kind! Please do not be confused. You must in fact see the big difference here, so that you may cultivate and foster a true rebirth, abandoning the hold that the mermaids have on you."

"What about demons? Do they exist? What is their nature and how do they function?"

"There is one demon that I uncovered just last night. There are many beings that are described as demons but they are in fact not. There is one though, that has been able to wreck havoc in my life for a very long time. I finally caught it last night, I confronted it, and then I banished it.

"Incredible! Tell me more!"

"This demon was able to hide within my perceptions of people who are dear to me, thus wrecking havoc between me and those whom I care about. It followed me around my whole life, taking its life from my perceptions of my loved ones and friends. Between the distance of myself and my loved ones, there is the void where perceptions are formed. This void of perception-forming exists between every person on this planet. It is a vital force, it is the jugular vein in the neck of relationships. This is where the demon attaches itself, sucking on the vein, a true vampire! It attaches and feeds on this vein by embodying the imaginations that you carry about someone after you have spoken to them, after you have encountered them, after a conversation, a get-together, a dinner, a gathering… when you are thinking about them, and wondering what that look must have meant or what that word must have meant. That form of energy-molding in the mind, is akin to a baby being conceived. In fact, it is the equivalent of a baby being conceived, in the spirit world. This is where that vampire attaches, because that energy you are molding in your mind is a vital force of life, the very first energies conceived during the formation of a bond with another. The doubts, the fault-finding, the ill-intentions, the deception, the evil motives, the destruction and the detraction— these images embodying your friends and your loved ones, that cause you to feel used, threatened, manipulated, harassed and shortchanged— these are actually the energy-hijackings of that demon. The demon wears their skin and attacks you in their form, as if it is they who harbor this negativity, this poison, towards you! That is the effect of this evil force harvesting the beautiful energies of spiritual birth in the form of mental perceptions of others.

"How did you uncover this demon after such a long time suffering from its afflictions? And more importantly, how did you banish it?"

"Last night, I was fighting the usual battle that I have been fighting and losing for so long now. I fought my dark perceptions about someone whom I love. The darkness arose within me like tsunamis, overwhelming all the memories of wonderful things that I love about this person, and I became consumed with doubt about his intentions, consumed with rage over the actions that I began to see as vile actions against me. So fast did the tsunami within me rise, and so fast did the light go away. I could no longer remember the reasons why I trusted this person, why I believe in him and why I need him. I only wanted to push him away, to run far away, and to cause him as much pain as he had caused me! I sometimes suffer from this darkness that has afflicted me and it has made me feel powerful to afflict the pain I have felt, onto the one who, in my mind, has caused me such deep pain!

But last night, I was determined to overcome it. Somehow, there was a flicker of a light in me that called out from within me, that screamed out his name, reminding me of his name, reminding me that I didn't want anything bad to ever happen to what I share with this man. At first, I wrote one angry, hurtful letter in a response to the darkness that pulsated through the atoms in my mind. Then I looked at the words on the paper, and while reading those words, I battled with the darkness by reminding myself of all the reasons why he didn't deserve to hear any of it. I threw away that letter and I wrote a different one, not as hostile as the first, but still venomous nonetheless. I then stared at the words, and, like the first time, I reminded myself of all the reasons why he didn't deserve that venom. Suddenly, the words didn't look justified, they didn't look real. I threw that letter away and I wrote yet another one, and another one, and another one! I wrote many letters, until I finally found him— the real him— inside of my heart, and underneath all of that rejection, resentment, doubt and vengeance that had welled up in my mind.

At the heart of me, at the root of us, I saw that there was a problem, and that problem was that I once gave him a gift that he didn't like. After that, I gave him another gift and he still didn't like it. I found in the heart of me, and at the root of us, that I did not need to persecute him for a million other things that were taking place in my mind. I only needed to tell him about the two gifts and how they made me feel rejected because he didn't like them. He didn't even know that they were gifts, because they were symbolic gestures and he didn't understand them. He did not realize that they were gifts for him and that fact was obvious in my mind.

I reached into my soul to find the words, to describe the scenario of what happened. It is difficult to do that because the demon attached to the jugular will tell you that if you expose yourself like that, you are weak and you will be laughed at, ridiculed. But I did it anyway, and I did it in gentleness and in whispering words.

That is when the demon appeared before me in my mind. I saw my spirit sitting by a pond, peaceful on a marble bench. The demon, not knowing that its form had already been exposed by the layers of words that I wrote down and then threw away, attempted to inflict the same venom that it is so used to injecting into my veins. It came groveling at my feet; a persuasive darkness permeated my skin at the touch of its hands, as it slithered like a snake and mimicked the man whom it had tried to embody for so long now. I looked it straight in the eyes, and said to it, 'I see you now! You are not him! None of them were ever you! It was always you, all along! It was never them!'

As I spoke to its face, it stood up and stumbled backwards, it kept on stepping backwards while still facing me, I commanded those at my right hand to hold it in place, where I proceeded to speak to it, to banish it from my past, present, future, and from my bloodline and from all my loved ones in this life and in all the other lives to come! I banished it into nonexistence. Then I took a wooden stake and drove it through the demon's heart.

A house then appeared and it was infested with black mold and mildew that had already hardened and crusted over like tar. It was the house built by these demon creatures, it was not my own house, but it was the house that they brought me to whenever they wanted to separate me from myself. I spoke out with authority, and I destroyed the house, I burned it, I banished it into nothingness along with all the creatures of darkness that built it! I was enraged at them! They, for so long, caused me to feel rage for the people in my life, when all along, the rage should have been directed at them!"

"So, there are demons, and they may be defeated just as one may defeat a vampire. I understand this now. What a dark and evil part of life, what a dark and vile existence that festers in our reality! Was it very difficult to peel back the layers of this demon and to reach within your heart of hearts, to grab onto the root, and to sweeten the root?"

"It was tremendously difficult. It was so difficult, that I don't believe I could have done it without the love that this man has for me. Once a vampire has latched onto your jugular, it is the most difficult suffering in the universe to overcome, the most difficult suffering to banish."

"Do vampires latch on so easily and so very often? How do these demons come about, and why is it that they are more pronounced in others than in some? Why do some suffer more and others suffer less?"

"Some of us had more negative experiences with people in our lives, some of us had a more tumultuous past. Our defense mechanisms are highly reactive due to our need to protect ourselves. That is the key ingredient in our bloodstreams that other people just do not have. It is therefore understandably much easier for this demon to latch onto those who are already susceptible to the fear of rejection due to past experiences.

Herein lies the great injustice of life: that our futures cannot be blamed on our pasts, meanwhile, we cannot choose to whom we are born, cannot choose our childhoods, and we never asked to be victims of the circumstances that once lay waste of us. In this sense, life has no mercy upon people. If you desire for future experiences far detached from your past experiences, then you must make it so. The effort you give will be greater than the effort given by others, but that is just how it is.

These demons are the outcomes of the negativity that surrounds the painful experiences we've been through, or that the people of the world have been through, in general. People would call them ghosts, but I do not call them ghosts. They are the remnants of experienced darkness in life."

"Are you telling me that when I am angry or when I am upset, this is all just demonic activity and my feelings are baseless and irrelevant?"

"Absolutely not. Do you think that I am crazy? That I would be filled with rage for no reason, that negative thoughts would haunt me for no rational reason? The rationality is there. But darkness has a way of taking the rational and giving it a different meaning. The reasons are rational. Then what is rational becomes poisoned by the injection of the feelings of rejection, fear, jealousy, doubt… it is not evil to be angry; however, your anger must not blind you from all of the good, from all of the Light! Your anger must not be so that it turns into rage! And your rage must not be so that it becomes the product of hate! Anything that happens to you is something that you may see by way of Light, or by way of darkness. And the proof would be rational in both the darkness *and* the Light! You *do* hold the power of creation, to create your reality. What I am telling you is that I do not want you to have an anger that blinds you to the good which is in your hands, your heart, your life.

Of course, there are circumstances that are entirely negative, that one may not look at by way of light, anymore. There are negative people who do negative things to intentionally hurt and destroy. These may not be seen by way of the light, these must be seen plainly for what they are— products of negative darkness. And I do believe that some people do not even possess human souls, but in fact possess souls of different origins. Some of those origins are insurmountably dark and must be avoided.

I am in no way telling you that your feelings are invalid, but I am saying that your feelings are often deceived, often sucked on by vampires. There are many situations and many people that are not nearly as horrible as you may understand them to be. That is a catastrophe in itself, for that is what would keep you away from love, all kinds of love."

"What is brightness? What is light? What does it mean when a person shines brightly?"

"When a light shines bright, a candle burns brightly, a flame roars in its serene original existence; the other lights, candles and flames think that the brighter one is going to kill them. But I have observed that this is a very limiting thing to think and to feel. And I have also learned that when you are a brightly-shining candle, your every smile and movement and thought and action is magnified— not because you magnify it and not because you are loud, but only because what is Bright will be Bright. And that's it. You have to realise your brightness, because it is when you lose sight of how much you shine that you will begin to hurt others with your Light. You don't realise the impact that you have, because you're thinking lower of yourself. You see, sometimes humility is actually the act of the acceptance of your greatness. You reach a point where it dawns on you that you have to stop saying, 'I'm not good enough, I'm not this or that enough, I'm just like this…' and you need to stand up straight into your full figure, into your full height, accept your stature— that is actually an act of humility. It is humble to accept that you don't have control over how much Light you were meant to shine into this world, and that if you are meant to be a gigantic Roman Candle, then so be it! I have seen those who have stood up into their full statures, into their full heights, and they appear as though they could break down a tree with a single glance! But all they've really done is *accepted*.

I am one of those people. But it took me too long to accept, too long to be humble; I ran away from myself for too long! I have never hurt another whilst in the knowledge of my Light; but, I hurt many whilst not accepting it, during the times that I was ignorant of it! And it is important to know that Brightness is not there to kill everything else around it. Brightness is not something that we need to compete for or that we need to chase after. But when one is Bright and Light, may we all stop for a minute to worship!"

"What made you finally Light Up? How did you come to finally accepting your Brightness?"

"At first I wanted to know that I could be everything, and that I could be everything fully and truly. And so I became everything, because I wanted to know that I could and because I wanted to actually be everything. I became a goddess, I became a human, I became an angel, I became a demon. I became darkness and I became the Sun, I became the sunlight and I became the snow. I became the rage and I became the whisper; I became the hunter and I became the hunted. I became the vampire, I became the princess. I became all, and I became all fully, and better than anyone else. I could, and I did. I knew that I could only truly choose who I am and what I am after first becoming everything.

One day, the Light entered me and saved me from mundaneness, saved me from weight, from gravity, from death. In those moments, on that day, I saw and I knew that Light is what gives you back your original wings, the wings that you had but you have already forgotten. A century worth of darkness is brought to absolutely nothing by a thread of light running along your spine, through your heart, taking root in your mind and blossoming upon your face! There is nothing that Light cannot conquer, and so, I chose to be This. I chose to Light Up. I chose an incredible lightness of being. I chose to light up the street, the city, the air, the face, the heart, the room, the home, the mind! There was no other option left— only this one. Because I chose this One over all the others. I have known all, and I have chosen One. I will Light Up, always, I will Light Up. The Light saved me, and it may stay in me, to build a home in me, a house in me, the Light may shine in me, forever and always. It chose me, and I chose it. We chose each other."

"How can we have the power to choose to Light Up? It must not be a simple task to choose? Considering the amount of darkness that is all around… how does one gain the power to choose The Light?"

"When someone believes in you while you are overcome by darkness and sees good in you and loves you despite your darkness; this gives you the power to choose the Light. When your darkness is accepted, it may finally rest in peace, and you may then simply choose Light. I am not saying that this is always the case, and I am not saying that this must always be the case. But if you do step into darkness, to know it fully, it is very difficult to simply step out again. But when someone looks at it and sees that it is beautiful still, that you are beautiful still, this *does* give you the power to choose the Light. I am also not saying that all who are loved in their darkness will choose to Light Up. Many will choose darkness. But I, and you— you and I do choose *Light*. Because it is above the mundane, it is too light for gravity to hold onto, it is above rot and remorse and reason. It just is. I am just I."

"How is it possible that you have known darkness but have not been corrupted by it?"

"Oh, I *was* corrupted by it. I lost belief in hope, in kindness, in faith, and in charity. You never know that you are corrupted, until you are no longer corrupted. Corruption cannot see itself. It must be seen by standing far away and then looking back at it.

But I think what you are really asking, is how I was not *destroyed* by it. To answer that is simple. Throughout everything that I became— wicked or good— I remained a child, always. There is a special provision for the child heart. The child heart may never be destroyed. In all things, I remained a child. When I lost the Light, I was a child of the Night. As for mercy… I did lose mercy bestowed upon me… my enemies grew stronger and stronger and I begged the Heavens for mercy, but there was none. And yet, all of that has become nonexistent, it has become nothing at all, only because I rose up into my stature and I Lit Up! A century of darkness may be escewed by a few moments of Sight! To See, then to Stand, then to Know. And the century is laid to rest, is crucified, is buried, is laid to waste, and still, no time has been taken from you, no day has been lost. This is the Power of Light.

In my dream last night, there was a witch's house, I tread ever so carefully because it was full of delicate, beautiful things and I was not aware that she was a witch! I accidentally broke a glass perfume bottle and I felt so sorry for my mistake, but then I noticed that she changed the bottle into another bottle, and enticed me to open the new one; but when I did, it broke again! So she changed it and enticed me again, and I yet again I broke the new one! After this third time, I then realised that I must stand up, rise up, and Light Up! I was not a prisoner of this house, or of this witch, or of this ever-deceptive perfume bottle! I would not be tricked! And so I went around her house, and I freed the many creatures she kept captive there; creatures which she had created from the darkness! I said, 'I banish all the darkness in you, I banish this creature of darkness and I in its place form a new creature of Light.' And there I crafted with my hands, my words, and with the air around me— formations and small spirits of Light; after nullifying their dark forms. And then I arose with wings so long, so wide and so strong, with these wings I arose into the sunset, I flew over the house of the witch and beyond it, there were no wires or posts to get into my way! It was only the sunset and I!

You must always, *always* remember, that Light nullifies darkness and it is for this reason that if you are born a very Bright and Shining Light, there will be much resistance by the darkness raised against you. They are struggling for their own lives, you see, for their own existence. But to cling unto the Light is to rise High Above those objects, those items that are of heavy darkness. We think that the key is to fight; but it is not, because the key is to Rise Above, to *float above! To fly!* The element of Light is Air— you must remain in that element of Air and float above, fly above. Rise Up, Light Up."

"Why is it so easy for you to use the word 'worship'? Is this not a sacred word, a word reserved only for sacred times?"

"I use the word 'worship' because I am easily brought into the state of worship. It is not the goal of sanctity to be aloof or to be seldom found! Do you think that sanctity wishes to only be called by its name, once in a while? What is wrong if you call her name often? Would this be a blasphemous thing? Since when is it a blasphemy to find and to seek the Divine in many things? If I were to see the face of the one whom I love, in the sunsets that I look at and in the dawn mornings that I gaze upon, would that be a blasphemy? When we see that which we love, often and in many beautiful things, is this a disrespect? I think not! So if the Dawn and the Dusk can call my heart into a state of worship, would that be any less respectful compared to the very Throne of God calling me unto the same? If I were to see the Divine in another person and that were to call me unto worship, should I not use the very word that describes what stirs within me?"

"But why see the Divine in many things? Is it not a blasphemy to reduce what is Magnificent down to what is mundane?"

"The rainbow is magnificent, and yet I may find the rainbow upon little spots of sunbeams through the window in my room. The five hundred year-old tree is magnificent, and yet, I may contemplate upon its wisdom and upon all that it has seen, while holding one of its leaves at the edge of my fingers.

The sunlight is magnificent; without it, humans and trees and flowers would cease to exist. And yet, I cannot gaze upon the Sun itself, but I must gaze upon the paintings of the Sun that are cast upon the Earth! The Earth is mundane while the Sun is Magnificent. If I am to seek and to adore the paintings that the Sun bestows upon the Earth, would that make me disrespectful of the Sun? Would that make me blasphemous? I think not, and I believe you and nobody else would think so!"

"Anybody who would think othwerwise, is an error of a person!"

"Indeed, and there are many such errors in the world right now. For some reason, people are taught that the scarcity of Divine Presence somehow increases its value! How so? If I were to give you more rainbows in your sky every day, would this decrease the value of the rainbow? And if I were to give you more Love in your life, would this decrease the value of my Love for you? To increase what is good, is to decrease what is good? How so? How is humankind taught such a way? And how is it that humankind accepts such a way? If I were to turn my back upon joy, upon laughter, upon the attainment of my heart's beautiful desires, will this somehow increase my holiness? Bring me closer to God? If I were to find and to see God less and less in the world when I look around at the sunlight and the flowers and when I inhale the scents so fine of cinnamon and of anise— if I were to abolish my desires of many things, in favour of seeing most things as being detached from God and apart from God— this is somehow supposed to make me holier? If I deny myself Beauty and Happiness in this life, because I ought to cast myself down as not being worthy of these things in the presence of God— this is somehow supposed to make me godly? If I see my flesh and bone as a sin, this is somehow supposed to raise my eyes to the true heights of the Divine? Now *this*— this is blasphemy! All of that, *that* is blasphemy! They take the word 'holy' and they place this word upon the foreheads of those who deny themselves and see themselves unworthy; they take the word 'divine' and they stamp this word onto the foreheads of those who bow their heads in many imagined shames; they take the word 'godly' and they engrave this word upon those who would deny themselves goodness and Beauty of this world in favour of the goodness and beauty that is imagined to become attainable after death— *that*— that is blasphemy! To teach a man to think as if he is dead, while he is still alive— *that* is a great evil!

"But I thought that we are to overcome the ego…"

"Why? Do you think that to overcome the ego means to overcome comfort, laughter and bliss? Do you think that to overcome the ego means to see your flesh as something defiled and merely mortal? Alas, the ego is not the presence of comfort, but the inflated ego thrives in the absence of the knowledge of comfort. True, there are many of those who live comfortably who have gratified egos, but it is not the presence of comfort; rather, the lack of the knowledge of comfort and its meaning, which forms the environment wherein the ego thrives. The ego does not know that the Soul is truly loved; the ego does not acknowledge that the Body is truly honoured; the ego is defensive by nature, and tells the Mind always that it is shortchanged, tells the Heart always that it is wronged! This is the ego— the absence of Bliss!"

"What is the best virtue to have?"

"I am tired of my virtues, I think I have too many of them!"

"If there is only one virtue that you would keep— just one— what would it be?"

"If I were to keep but only one virtue, that would be the virtue of Humility. Without Humility, I feel like there is a dense cloud stranded atop my face, refusing to go away! I feel like I am a puffiness, a puffed up, unattractive thing that doesn't know when to turn left and doesn't know when to turn right! And I am not talking about the type of humility that others say they have, when they 'lower themselves' down for all to see. That is not Humility! In the first place, Humility never lowers anyone! Humility is what removes that dense cloud from before your face and allows your inner Sun to shine and your inner Moon to glow! Humility is what removes the unattractive puffiness from your body and covers you in attractive feathers, allowing you lightness of being, giving you the winds to fly! Before all things and above all things— grow a Rose of Humility within your soul. And not the kind of humility that wants to show that it is good or that it is virtue; rather, the kind of Humility that, through its mere presence, increases the value of the valuable and exposes the truth in pretension. I'm talking about Humility as powerful as the most powerful weapon— grow that kind."

"How may I grow that kind of Humility? Tell me how!"

"This kind of Humility— true Humility, which is power— is grown through much painful denial of the sudden impulses of ego. There are things that you want to do, you want to say, because it will gratify your ego. The reactive nature that stands in between Soul and Body— that one in the middle— it wants to react to everything that happens to it, in order to defend itself, as if everything is designed to belittle it, to tread on it… go ahead and tread on and belittle it. It must be flattened so that strong bridges may be built across it, so that Body and Soul may both rise and luminate, together! That is power, and that power is attained and maintained, through Humility. Humility is love, it is Love of the Self. To Love yourself so much, that you are willing to crumble down and to flatten the very part of you that falsely says that it is your Self— to do this on behalf of your True and Pure Self— this is a sacrifice of Love. To be humble is to Love yourself thoroughly, and to Love thoroughly those whom are given you to love.

Deny your sudden urges to figure out when you have been shorthand, to witch-hunt those who have wronged you and by what words they have wronged you; your urges to make sure that no one and that nothing is stealing what is rightfully yours— let go of that. Overcome by letting go. Through this, you will attain Humility that is Power.

And remember, that in all things, you must not set your mind to judge what any other is doing or saying or thinking. That is their own. In judging others, you effectively detract from yourself, while no harm comes to those whom you have judged!"

"Why is it that so many relationships fall through and so many partnerships and marriages crumble and disappear?"

"The answer to that is simple. People's relationships fall because they do not understand the reason for having a relationship. One is there because she has something he wants and the other is there because he has something she wants, and they are attracted to one another, so why not stick around for a while? People aren't there to be the other person's partner, anymore. They don't even know what being a partner means!

I told a man once, I said, 'I hope that the times I am wrong are the times that you are right.' And that is what being a partner in life means. That is what having a relationship means. It means being there for each other, being strong for the other when he or she is weak, it means protecting one another and knowing that you are on each other's side! It means being right when the other is wrong and it means having someone right when you are wrong. I told him, I said, 'I want my wrongs to have a right... you know? Because otherwise, it's just all wrong.' And that's what it means to *be* with someone. How can other people have that, when they are too busy competing with one another and playing games with each other, each one trying to make sure that he/she doesn't get shorthanded in the relationship!

People do not stay in love, because they do not know how to love. They do not know Humility, they do not know what it means to give themselves to another, to their partner. They do not know.

Therefore, what they do not know— they cannot have!"

"And why are so many people not faithful in their relationships? Why is it so easy for some to cheat on a person they profess to love?"

"So many people cheat because they put themselves into situations wherein it is easy for them to cheat. They feel like the meaning of 'being faithful' is 'not feeling like cheating'. They don't know that the meaning of faithful is, 'not putting oneself in the situation where one might not be faithful.' They think their relationship is some kind of a game— they think they can see how far they can go before they feel like sleeping with someone new!"

"Really? Do people really think like that?"

"Yes, it is amazing, isn't it? And I am glad to see that you are surprised by this, too."

"It seems all too stupid for anyone to actually think that way!"

"But, alas, millions of people think that way!"

"To be faithful is to decide to begin to make decisions in your life, on a daily basis, that will support your desire to be faithful."

"I know that without even needing to ask you."

"Yes, you do. And, you are right. My faithfulness to my partner begins on the day that I begin to make decisions on a daily basis that incorporate the support of my desire to stay with my partner, to be loyal to him, and to experience a thriving relationship with him. To be faithful, I will not put myself knowingly into a circumstance where game-playing begins, I will not put myself knowingly into a situation that I know is not conducive for the strengthening of our relationship. And this is how we are faithful, this is how we can stay faithful. It is through decisions made in the mind, it is through thought process, it is through intuition, sensing, and the anticipation of what might become of any given situation in a day. The faithful partner is constantly weighing possible outcomes of actions taken. And perhaps that is precisely why many people get tired of being faithful— because to be faithful, your senses and

your mind must be awake! To be faithful, your
intuition must be either very loud; or you must listen
to it very closely. To be faithful is to walk each day
through the world illuminated from within, like a
bioluminescent thing from the bottom of the sea! All
your nerves must come to life, to guard the love that
you share with another, to protect what you share
with another, to keep what you share with another.
It is not something you may do part-time, or half-
time, or just when you 'feel like it'!

People fail at their endeavours, when they act
like all things are to be carried out according to how
they feel in the moment, instead of according to what
they actually want. Please make this distinction—
that what you want is not necessarily what you
sporadically feel in a certain moment. What you
want is what you want for ten years from now, for
twenty-five years from now, and for the rest of your
life. *That's* what you want! And yet, people make the
error of putting themselves, so many times, into
positions that are capable of pulling them away from
what they want, on the basis of what they feel like in
a given moment.

People are no longer making decisions to stay together no matter what. And that is why so few are faithful."

"What is the value of living a happy life with a partner? And what is the value of living a happy life, generally, whether or not you are spending it with your other half?

"In this world, there is both Heaven and Hell. You ought to know this, because when you do not know this, you're not going to be aware that things could in fact be hell for you! And when you are not aware of all the tragedy and depression and sadness in this world, then you are not going to do everything in your power (and even beyond your own immediate power), to move towards Joy, Peace, Serenity, Abundance, Fulfillment, Happiness! Because that is what you *should* do! You really *should* do everything in your power to move earnestly into the direction of the Beautiful Gifts! And when moving into that direction is beyond your power, you should call on all Higher Powers that be! From the earliest, soonest place in your life, where you are able to build things, to decide upon things and to make choices towards things for yourself, it is integral and it is important that you build and do and move in the ways that will create the Beautiful Gifts for you and for those whom you love! We create our Heavens and our Hells here on Earth, and we must know that there is a Hell, because if not, then we will instead choose to float around; playing around and toying with sadness and depression, loneliness and tragedy… don't! Do not play around and tempt those things into your life! Don't you know that they are real? They are real and they are terrible. But you may remove them from your reality— do that! Remove them from your reality. Do not toy with them as ideas or as points of interest or 'spices' in life! They are not spices! They are small hells!

As much as possible, create reasons to laugh! As much as possible, build reasons to enjoy and to celebrate! As much as possible, create moments of comfort, of affection and of mirth. As much as possible, make your days festive and fulfilling. Each and every day! Make *each day* a festive fulfillment of Joy and of Peace! And accept Love into your life!

Too many people do not accept Love into their lives, as if Love comes along every day, as if it is popcorn— something cheap and fun! But everyone knows that it is *not* popcorn, it's *not* easy to come by! And yet, so many people let it come and go and don't grab onto it. *Don't* be one of those people!

Life is too short not to be obsessed over something or someone. People have mastered the art of crafting a life that floats on top of the water, because they are afraid of drowning in the depths. But is that even a life, is that even living? Or is that just called being a living organism surviving on a planet called Earth? Life is too short not to drown in the dark waters of what it means to have a life. Why don't we let another person consume us so fully and so brutally, so that when we die one day, we will never die alone; we will in fact die with one half of another's soul inside of us! Or why don't we let something consume us so fully and so brutally, so that when we die one day, we will never really die because our legacy will live on! Drown, I say, drown! Drown in this life until you are so dead, that death won't even bother with you! Drown in this life until you are so dead, that you make death look like a speck in the sunlight. Drown until you are so alive, you won't need any other lifetime but this one."

"Is there a due amount of respect that we must have for this world? We see the dirt and the mud, we wish to mold that into gold; we see the darkness and the soot, we wish to transform that into petals and into diamonds. But I wonder, is there a need to respect any of it? Any of it at all? For just the way that it is?"

"This is my answer for you: Give to Caesar what belongs to Caesar. You are in the world, be a light in the darkness, not a dog who barks in the darkness. Give to Caesar what is Caesar's. You are in the world, be a beacon of love, not only a dreamer of dreams. Give to Caesar what belongs to Caesar, you have your own way in the world; but others have their own, too.

"But what does that mean?"

"Caesar represents the dominions of this world, and the idea is not to become a dog barking at the darkness in the world (many dominions in the world are made of darkness); but the goal is to be the light in the darkness, the light is *not* a barking dog filled with rebellion or with rage. The light is a gentle being, it is something that just is, it is something that just shows and guides and leads.

Caesar represents the kingdoms of this world, some are dark while others are light. It is not up to us to determine the kingdoms that God has put in the world, but it is ours to act upon Love and not only dream up dreams. Many are dreaming of better, many are dreaming of more or of different; but the most powerful force that will be able to make those move, is Love!

Caesar represents the leadership in this world that we may or may not approve of. And though many struggle against the leadership, resulting in anarchy and rebellion, you must know that what is Caesar's should be given to Caesar— while you make your own path. If there are those who would join you on your path, then that is great! But if others do not join you, do not think that they are lost! They are on their own path! You be the Jacob who dreams of the Ladder. And you may climb that Ladder, never to look back. But not all are meant to dream of that Ladder, to find it, nor to climb it. It is not our task to set the world free from the paths that she is on. It is only our task to know our own paths, and then to take them. Anything more is a good measure in excess and should be a reason for gratitude, but not a goal."

"How are we to create balance in this world? Surely you believe in balance, yes? They say that balance is created by those who have more, when they give to those who have so much less. The more giving to those who have less is how balance is created in this world, that is what they say."

"The mere fact they are saying that what creates balance is when those who have more give to those who have less, is evidence of their misunderstanding and ignorance of what balance is. So if you are more beautiful than someone, does this mean you must suffer more in this life, be put through more difficult trials in this life, be made to endure more cruelty in this life, because you are more beautiful while the other person is not? If you were born rich, does this mean that you are deserving of more suffering than the one who was born poor? Taking from those who have more, or pulling down those who have more, is not the key to balance! The only result of that is all of you will go down, together! How is that balance? You are thinking of a balance scale, you see, and this is the great flaw in your method of thinking. Allow me to explain— when you put a heavier weight on one end, with a lower weight on the other end, there will be an imbalance and the pan with the heavier weight will go down, while the pan with the lesser weight will go up. This image in itself, puts your logic at flaw. This logic would state that those who have more will fall on their own, anyway, and that the more that they have, the lower that they will fall! Therefore, taking from them would only slow down their fall, and slow down your ascent (assuming, for example, that you are the lesser one, the complainer of inequality). Therefore, if you would like to speed up your ascent, then it would only make sense if those who have more, would be given even more! That way, the more gold is in the pan— the faster you fly higher and the faster they fall lower! So as you can see, this logic in itself is contradictory and detrimental.

Now, let's look at the balance scale again. In order to create a steady and unwavering balance between the two pans on either side, equal proportions need to be placed on each pan. So, equal amounts of gold would need to be placed on each side, in which case, nobody will ever get better. And if we always put more gold and equal amounts of gold in each pan, there is no flying higher, for either side. Is this what is wanted? A constant mundaneness? What becomes of a constant state of mundaneness while there is no reason to reach, to fly, and to attain? You can answer that question, yourself. The answer is obvious.

We do not create balance by wishing and inflicting evil upon those who have more. Envy is the root of all evil; envy, and its effects, such as resentment, are not the solutions to attaining balance in this world. But when those who have more, *willingly share* with those who have less, this increases the act of generosity in the world, and *generosity is the engine of balance*.

There are two types of equalities that are being attempted in the world, as we speak. One type is benevolent while the other type is malevolent. The one is an equality that seeks to improve everyone and everything, thereby lifting up humanity unto a higher place, as a whole. Then there is the equality that seeks to level down everything for everyone, thereby reducing what is better, in order to to match what is wounded, what is hurting… there is such a thing as too much empathy. There is such a thing as too much seeking out to feel the pain of others, to the point that we will allow pain to be inflicted where pain is not present, in a bid to 'be one' with the hurting; in an attempt to 'feel with' those who are wounded and in pain. This is an altogether misused form of empathy! Empathy is there so that we may feel exactly the hurt of another and exactly the joy of another, in order to alleviate the hurt and to bring out the joy! Now, when empathy is applied as a means to transport the demise of the few, on to becoming the demise of the many, in order to create a certain twisted form of 'oneness'— this is already a misconstructed empathy, a form of brainwashing of the massess, a kind of change in favour of the shitholes of this world, it is absolute madness. It is absolute madness to destroy the banqueting tables, in order to match the hunger. It is absolute madness to annihilate the happiness in order to match the sorrow. It is absolute madness to take from those who have, in order to level them down to those who have not. If one is to *give* to those who have not, in order to improve their lives, may it be in such a way that it will not cause the giver to suffer a lack! Do not shoot down the birds in order to feed the hyenas! I place emphasis on *give,* because, the word should not be *take.* Do not take from others, that is called theft! But allow others to give out of kindheartedness, and only to the amount that will not inflict a lack or a loss on their end. Never demand more than that and never accept more than that. Do not alter the physics of the balancing scale, do not destroy the banqueting tables.

There is perhaps in this day and age, a strange type of communism— a neo-communism— which intends to equalize everything for all, through taking away from those who have more. But it becomes strange and it becomes novel in this day and age, because it is applied with good quality traits (empathy, compassion, sympathy and the like). One must become so compassionate, that one should let go of one's own, for the sake of the other; one must become so sympathetic, that one must put as second her own family and her own life, in favor of the family and the life of another. There is a false application of oneness, of equality, that is being applied through good qualities— something like a beautifully wrapped communism. The frightening thing is that it is very rampant and very effective amongst the masses, today."

"Generosity is the engine of balance?"

"Yes. Generosity is the engine of balance."

"How then, may we produce generostiy amongst those who have more, in order to generate balance in our world?"

"Certainly not by labelling them and crucifying them! Those who are hurt are seldom kinder as a result! I used to give so much more, before I was hurt! Then when I was hurt by the hands of envy, I gave less, and thought of my own welfare more!

We must all understand that those who do have more, also have their own stories to tell though they do not often tell them. It is never true that everything was wonderful and that nothing ever hurt! Even those whom you envy have their own stories and they have their own hurts. Also, those who have more must understand those who have less, for they have their own stories, too, and obviously, their own hurts. But those who have more, are not predetermined by Destiny to understand more, to give more. Often, it is those who sit around judging the ones who have more, that will fall, and this of course creates an even greater imbalance in the world. It also creates a greater imbalance within individual people, because, the one who already has less becomes corrupted by his/her own envy, and thus, comes to possess even lesser as a result.

May those who have more understand and be kind to those who have less, and may those who have less understand and be kind to those who have more. Equal amounts of understanding given, and equal amounts of kindness given, is what will produce the much sought-after and elusive thing called, *equality*. All must give in equal proportions— of those things which money cannot buy, those things called understanding and kindness— herein is the act of generosity, herein is the generator engine of equality! In giving equal proportions of those virtues that money cannot buy, equality is produced in this world.

When people talk about inequality, they think primarily on the inequality that exists with regards to monetary wealth— that this is the main reason of failure in society, in the world, in life in general. But the truth is that, inequality exists in many other areas, as well. There is a great inequality that exists in families (between happy ones and dysfunctional ones), a great inequality that exists between people as individuals (some are born with many talents, others none),and so on and so forth. The disproportionate distribution of money is not the only circumstance that creates unequal opportunity for people.

You cannot choose to be born of better health, of better love, of better care, of better happiness… things that often are not a result of either the presence or the absence of money. The most fundamental nanoparticle of any nation is the family unit, and then the children. There should be people striving to create equal opportunity for children to be born to parents that love them just as much as the most loved children of the world. There should be people striving to create equal opportunity for couples to fall in love with one another, all of them, just as much as the most love-stricken couples in this world! When people are more successful in their family lives— those people should be giving away their know-how, giving away their knowledge of how they attained that success. When people are more successful raising their children, they should share that wealth with others, so that others may become better at raising good children, too. When people are overcomers, overcoming the hardships in life, they should share that inner strength with others so that others may learn to become victorious in mind and in heart, too! These are the wealths, that when shared, are not diminished! To share and to give from these types of wealths does not mean to diminish and to hinder what is your own. Therefore, there is no depletion that takes place within this type of giving (unlike when giving away money, which is a material and a limited source). It will not deplete and pull down your own, when you share from these prosperities.

But nobody will be equally happy, equally in love, equally talented, equally healthy... maybe some people are, but the time will never come when this will be equal for every single person on the face of this planet. Nevertheless, those are in fact the things that matter more than money. And so we have it, that there are those who focus all their attention onto creating equality in the financial aspect of the idea, saying that things must be equal because money is not as important— as this— as that— but they are contradicting themselves in the process, because, they put no effort into investing into love, into health, into children, into families, in order to create equality in the places where it matters the most.

Nothing is ever going to be equal for everybody, and that is because happiness is not equal, health is not equal… we cannot choose whom we are born to, where we are born, what stories our lives take form of. Inequality of the distribution of monetary wealth is the result of the inequality of love, of health, of talent, of care, of happiness. Those things are not the result of the inequality in the ownership or the stewardship of money. The inequality of money is the result of the inequality of those things. Money is the material thing, while the other things up there are not material, and what is not material, is what first occurs. There is degradation in the equality in economies, in finances— because there is degradation in the equality of happiness, love, and health in families, in people, in children, in the core ingredients that make a life. But these ingredients will never be the same for everyone, because none of us are the same!

But herein we are equal: in the fact that all of us are different. Herein we are equal: in the fact that none of us will ever be the same. Herein we are equal: in the fact that my desire to become, and to love, may be equal to your desire to become and to love. We may become all equal in our desires to see the good I want for me— be the good I want for you. The joy I want for me— be also the joy I want for that person over there! But still, this will be limited to desire, because, what is good for me, may not be what is good for that person over there; and what is joyous for me, may not be what is joyous for you. But the desire may be equal. And we may all one day recognize how others desire for their own good and for their own joy, and be able to identify that with our own.

The beauty in living, comes from the many different colors of it and if all of the colors were just the same, just one color, then life wouldn't even be worth looking at."

"What, then, will it take for this to happen? What, then, will it take for all parties to give equally of those things so priceless that money cannot buy?"

"Oh, it will take the reduction of the ego. The ego declares that each party is more deserving than the other, to receive of these things, and so, the ego holds back each party from freely giving these items. Ego tells each party involved, 'You deserve more understanding, you are the one who is on the losing end here, you are the one who is deserving of more kindness here, if you give these things right now, then you are going to be shortchanged.' And so, neither party gives freely. Generosity of priceless items is not produced. Equality is not generated."

"Is it then safe to say that equality will reign in this world only when ego diminishes or is removed entirely?"

"Yes."

"Who was Christ on this Earth?"

"Who was Christ on this Earth, but a man who dined with harlots and thieves? Who was Christ on this Earth, but a man who allowed a prostitute to bathe his feet in perfumes? Who was Christ on this Earth, but He who said, 'It is the stuff coming out of a man that defiles him; not the stuff going into him that ruins his heart.'

And yet what has the vain-hearted man turned this Christ into? He has turned this same Christ into a symbol of all hypocrisy and perfectionism. The vain hearted man has turned this same Christ into a symbol of all that cannot be attained! A symbol of struggle against Hell! He who swallowed Hell whole, has been turned into a symbol of war against sin. There is no war against sin; all sin was made void, because it is not what is on the outside that is seen by God; but it is what is on the inside that God sees! And even this simple principle has been catapulted into that which it does not even mean. Because they say what is on the outside does not matter, but then they take their vanities and hide them in an attempt to look like they do not even care! Where are their vanities hidden now? Their vanities are pushed under the covers, inside of their hearts.

Who did Christ sit and dine with? With those dressed in white robes; or with those whores dripping in gold earrings and pearls? Who did Christ sit with? With the Priests clad in white robes; or did he sit with the tax collectors? Christ sat with all manner of those who wore their vanities upon their own skin for all to see.

I cannot be fooled by those who speak of Christ but did not know Him. Who does not know Christ? Is it the holy Priest or is it the harlot who sat with him for his meals? Who does not know Christ? Is it the untainted Priest, the Pharisee; or is it the thief who hung beside him at the cross? They all claim to know Christ and to know what he is all about, and yet, would He sit with them if He were here? For their vanities, I tell you, their vanities they hide in their hearts."

"What is goodness, what is generosity? How can I know if I have goodness, how can I know if another has goodness and generosity? How can I identify it?"

"I think that a lot of the time, people are generous towards those whom they pity whilst only finding fault in those whom they see as better than themselves. There is a fake kind of goodness, that is the goodness that is only good towards other people that make the givers feel better about themselves. Would you be good to someone you think is so much better than you are? Or who has so much more than you have? Or is your goodness only reserved for those who make you feel like a God because you give to them? Too often, there are shining, beautiful people, who suffer so much in this world because there would be so many others willing to snuff out their flames. Goodness of a person is not measured by sympathy or compassion; rather, goodness is measured by empathy. Empathy goes beyond all the physical things you see with your two eyes. It's easy to be good to those whom you pity; much harder to be good to those whom you envy!

You have been raised with a mindset dictating that compassion and sympathy are the telltale factors of goodness in a man (or woman). We were all raised this way. But compassion and sympathy are qualities that are accompanied by pride, because you are aware that bending down makes you a good person. *Your ego is gratified.* Compassion and sympathy are also defined by the presence of lack. There can be no compassion if there is no lack, there can be no sympathy if there is no lack. Therefore, if you are to define your goodness based upon compassion and sympathy, then this means that your goodness only exists where lack exists, that your goodness requires a victim/victims in order to thrive!

Just look at any Facebook account, Google account, or Facebook Page! Everyone likes the Dalai Lama! And that's regardless of whether or not they actually understand Buddhism! Why do people want to be associated with the Dalai Lama? That's easy! That is because there is an instant gratification of being seen as a person with generous and kind ideals! It's not about actually living that way from the heart; it's about association with something that makes them look good! Of course, I'm not saying that every single person who likes Dalai Lama is like this, but I'm saying that I am aware of the fact that he is an actual person who is desirous of human connection, who shouldn't be used as a quick ego boost.

The act of yearning to be seen as a good person is a selfish act that does not come from the heart. Then what kind of goodness comes from the heart, you may ask. And why do I say that goodness is measured by empathy rather than by sympathy and compassion? That is because empathy is able to connect with another person, regardless of outward physical attributes. Empathy is what feels the pain of a person who's rich and powerful and doesn't need your help. Empathy is what feels the heart of another person who is beautiful, kind, happy and loved. Empathy goes beyond the physical stimuli that is responsible for evoking reactions and feelings; and instead, reacts to what is *really* going on inside of a person. People normally see only what the other people plainly show. But empathy is what sees beyond what is shown and connects with that.

How easy is it to be good to those who make you look good whilst you are being kind to them? Politicians do that all the time. Beauty Queens do that all the time. But can a politician be kind to his fellow politician who is more popular than he? Can a beauty queen be kind to her fellow contestant who is surely going to win over her? You see— this is how true goodness and character is measured. It is measured by the extent that one has gone out of one's area of self-comfort, in order to connect with another human being, in order to be kind to another human being. You see, kindness is not a clothing that we wear! Kindness, in fact, is a state of the heart, a state of the soul! Can you be kind to a person when you know they are going to be responsible for making you look not-as-good as they are? And because someone is responsible for making you look not-as-great as you would like to be seen, simply by being themselves, does that immediately equate to them being bad people? Or is it you who is the bad person, because you cannot allow yourself to be seen as any lesser than the way you want to be seen? Is it actually you who possesses the bigger ego in this case? I have learned many a time over, that it is often those who have lesser, who are the most arrogant and the most proud! Why? Because arrogance and pride is all that they really have to hold onto!

Very often, you will find a very good person wrapped behind a layer of thorns, not wanting to be seen as good! Not wanting to be known as kind! Why? Because they know that it hurts to be good and to be kind! Because people take advantage of those virtues and the reason why they have been hurt so much in life, is for the very reason that they *are* kindhearted, they *are* warmhearted, they *are* gentle! And yet, do we stop to see these people, to recognise and to validate these people? Hardly! We are too busy validating those who fit the moulds and the cookie cutter image of what it means to be a 'good person'!

Should people in this world be punished because they are more physically attractive, because they have been loved more, because their house is bigger? I don't think so. This is the same evil that causes poverty and shame and hardship in the world, because the evil that causes that is in itself of that nature, it does not actually matter *where* and *who* it is emanating from! When it comes from the rich— it destroys. When it comes from the poor— it destroys. The evil of destruction is of itself within its own nature and it may permeate anyone and any form that it likes.

You measure the goodness of another by the other's ability to forgive you, but look at yourself first! Whom have you not forgiven? You measure the goodness of another by the other's willingness to help you, but look at yourself first! How far would you actually go to help another? You tend to measure the goodness of another by what is done unto you, but do you measure your own goodness in the same way? Better yet, why measure the goodness in others, at all? Why not preoccupy yourself with measuring *yourself* instead of measuring others? Because the greatest work that is to be done, and that we can only actually really do, is the work upon ourselves. To find the faults in ourselves and to fix those. To find the cracks in ourselves and then to mend those. We are all carpenters, sculptors, masons, builders! But the greatest temple that we need to build is the temple within our own souls! And we cannot build our own temples when we are so preoccupied with how other people are building or not building their own!"

"I want to have true goodness within me, I want it to fester in me like a contagious disease! How can I cultivate goodness within myself?"

"Take upon you the eyes of true kindness— which is empathy— and connect with those whom you envy, those who have more than you do, those who make you feel lesser than what you are. Connect with those who are kinder, who are happier, who are gentler. Connect with someone who is more attractive, more talented. Find the person inside the individual that doesn't make you look good, and love that person. Or at least understand and feel that person. Cultivate real goodness, today."

"Can I be good even without abstinence? Even without living on top of a mountain, separate from others? Can I have true kindness and still have sexual desires? How can I become spiritual if I derive so much pleasure from the act of sex?"

"I find it funny how people view sex as something purely physical and animalistic in nature. Sex is never associated with innocence, is it not? Or with purity? But why? Why is it that in our minds, this act is never associated with innocence, purity and spirit? Why is it always categorised as 'lust', and lust categorised as 'animalistic', as only physical, as only material in nature?

When we think about religion today— for example, when we think about Christianity— we immediately think of sex being impure unless it is done in the confines of marriage. Funny. How can a holy religion cause a natural thing to become unholy? I am sure you have never heard that before and I am sure I have just opened your eyes right there (that's called gnosis). Think of this again: *How can a holy belief system cause a natural act to become unholy?* Can what is holy cause anything natural to become unholy? Is something holy if it can cast unholiness upon a natural act that is responsible for the continuation of the human race?

People ignorantly assume that Paganism treated sex as unholy and animalistic, but nothing can be further from the truth. The ancient belief systems now called 'Paganism', actually regarded sex as a holy act, in itself— responsible for the elevation of the spirit. And why not think that way? Why not believe that? The act that is responsible for the continuation of the human race, should in fact naturally be held in regard as also being responsible for the elevation and enlightenment of the spirit! What is the elevation and the enlightenment of the spirit? It is innocence. The more enlightened and elevated a soul is— the more childlike it is in nature!

It is entirely through a system of brainwashing that we have all come to regard the act of sex as something unholy unless you go to get papers done to say you can legally do it. Since when has paperwork made anything holy? Can papers filled out here on Earth make something holy for our Souls that come from the Eternal Place? Can what is below validate what is above? Is it the lesser that is responsible for uplifting the higher? In what insane existence is this so? Why is it that people believe that outward acts are responsible for the condition of their souls that are inside of them? It is in fact the condition of your soul that is inside of you, which produces the effect of the outward acts that you do! And do you know who said this? Jesus did!

We honour and we revere the act of sex, not only because it is the greatest pleasure that a human being is capable of experiencing, but because it is in fact an act that truly elevates the spirit and the soul. Of course, when you have sex with no gnosis, as dumb as a doorknob and as insentient as a nail, then this is the same thing as dogs copulating. But take note of this: *the effect is merely a result of the cause;* the cause being that the individual is already initially insentient! Therefore, an insentient individual with the sense of a nail, can only produce what is of his/her own nature. It is not the result that takes effect upon the cause! It is the cause (the initiator of the act) that is responsible for bringing forth the effect.

We honour and we revere the act of sex, not only when it is done in the confines of marriage as stated by major religions, but we honour and we revere the act of sex, because it is an act sacred to the human race. We bring new souls into the world through this act; we unite our soul with another through this act; we experience the most ecstatic of pleasures through this act. We honour the act shared between two people, as belonging to themselves. We honour and we revere their relationship, because it is a bond shared between the two. We honour marriage— yes we do. We honour people's relationships— yes we do. And we honour it even more, when we are awakened to the fact that it is a divine act, innocent in itself."

"You've told me about bringing new souls into the world… what are souls?… but what I really mean is, what is the relevance of human souls and of the variety of these that we bring into this world?"

"Not all souls are equal— this is the hard-to-swallow truth. But it is the truth, nonetheless. It is the nature of the soul that is responsible for both the filth in this world and for the Beauty in this world. Insentient souls produce all things damaging and horrific; sentient souls produce all things Beautiful and Divine. All human beings are sentient beings, but not all souls within human beings are sentient souls!

The same goes with sex! It is not the act of marriage that purifies sex and cleaves it unto innocence, but it is the state of the soul that does this! Impure souls, even within marriage, cannot produce spiritual elevation through sex! The lack of a marriage certificate is not going to be reason for a lack of soul bonds between partners who produce Beauty together.

Now, I am not saying that I am against marriage and I am not saying that I am against religion. I am not against anything; I am in fact only looking at the truth. How does one look at truth? One looks at truth by stepping outside of the range of vision that normal people are capable of seeing things in, and seeing EVERYTHING THAT IS TO BE SEEN. Truth is seen by eyes of eagles!

Why is lust any lesser, anyway? I should want to Love whom I Lust and Lust whom I Love! Why have people tried to separate their objects of desire from their objects of devotion? Cannot one desire what one is devoted to and also be devoted to what one desires? We are souls inside bodies, are we not? Cannot the Soul and the Body live in harmony and reverence one for the other? I think this is the way that it should be. What has religion done? Religion has only sought to separate the two, creating a vision within the mind that dictates one is worthy of hellfire while one is worthy of heavenly clouds. Preposterous! And so we are to worship a God who has put a heavenly thing within a hellbound thing? Who in their right mind would worship such a God? I do not believe that our bodies are hellbound while our souls are heavenbound! If there is any Divinity in me, then may it be all throughout me! The carnality, the hedonism, the purity, the innocence— this is all Divine, altogether! At least, in me I know it is!

Sex can be innocent, pure and ecstatic, all at the same time! It depends upon the condition of the souls involved. It is not a heinous act that must be purified by prison time; it is not an act of murder! It is in fact quite the opposite of that! Why must we, in our minds, separate our Lust from our Love? Why not let the two dance together? Why not respect both and thereby purify the deemed lesser material into what is pure and what is gold? If you think something is made of mere coal, then do not simply throw the coal to the side! Take the coal and make it into gold! And better yet— do not have any coal at all. But only filter everything through your filters of gold. And this is how you shall identify Holiness. Holiness is what is capable of purifying that which it touches!"

"So, you mean to say that Holiness is more powerful than those things that are unholy, than those things that are impure?"

"But of course! If Holiness were less powerful than unholiness and less effective than what is impure, then why would we even desire it? Why should one desire the thing that is less effective, that is less than the best? Is it not a noble act to desire the best state that man can be in? The best state is the state of Power, of Freedom, of Love! Do you think that what is powerful is to be shunned? Because that is not so! Love is powerful, Freedom is powerful, Innocence is very powerful! It's usually the things dubbed as less powerful that are actually more powerful in reality."

"What is Love? People ask this all the time, and they say it is the most difficult question for anyone to ever answer."

"They think that Love is a feeling, an emotion; but, it is not! Love is Power, Love is what gives you the Power to rise above your five senses and to rise above your emotions and your feelings, in order to stay on the track, in order to keep the pace, in order to keep something in sight… Love is what keeps. Love keeps you on a path, keeps you moving towards a vision, keeps you in a place, or keeps you moving on… Love brings you higher than your emotions and your feelings, giving you the power to direct your emotions and to direct your feelings, rather than to be directed by them. And yet, it is not separate from emotion, it is not separate from feelings, but it rises above. Similar to how the wave is not separate from the ocean; nevertheless, it is the wave that causes the motion of the ocean, it is the wave that rises above, it is the wave that creates movement, it is the wave that forms and dictates the direction of the ocean. So Love— Love is like a wave in the ocean— while everything else is the rest of the ocean. Love is Power, Love is direction, Love is where we go and how we get to it!"

"But tell me, how has it come to be, that the things that are actually of true Power, are now seen as less desirous in our times, today?"

"That is because we live in a world lacking Sight, lacking Vision, and lacking Belief. First of all, you are laughed at for believing in anything that most people don't believe in, so you lose you sense of belonging. Truths are out there beyond the limits of what most people believe in, so in the very act of going to what is beyond, you are already giving up your sense of belonging. This is very difficult to do, so that is why very few do it.

It is also a difficult and uncomfortable task to see more than what others see, because you are alone in seeing these things. You want to share a view of a mountain, of a brook, of a well-lit alleyway, of a sunset or a sunrise... you don't want to look at these things alone! But to see more than what others see, is to watch the sunset alone, is to view the sunrise alone. You cannot show people what you are looking at, when they are unwilling to look into those directions. Therefore, to see more and to watch more and to know more— is to live in the absence of sharing— and that is an absence that no one wants to live in.

Of course, you can still share what others don't want to look at; but then you will not be able to choose whom you share these with, you will have to simply put things out there, then the one who is willing will come. Many are called, but few are chosen. And you are not the one who is doing the choosing.

So as you can now see, people have not desired the greater and prized them as the more powerful, simply because they do not know. They do not see, they do not know."

"Do people even see their own Souls? Do they look at themselves and know who they are?"

"Much of the human Soul is tucked away within the dark recesses of the individual person. And the eyes are not trained, nor are they taught to see, those Elements of the Heart that thrive in those cracks and crevices. But they are not even always cracks and crevices; they are sometimes fine corners where all is covered in convenient darkness. The Philosopher's Stone is that which gives the eyes the Sight to see into these corners, beyond the convenient darkness that covers; the Philosopher's Stone is that which brings the eyes into those places, to look upon their own reflection and see the Soul within! It is sometimes just a glance; but it is at other times a long gaze. Nevertheless, the Philosopher's Stone is that which makes the darkness conscious of itself, because when the darkness becomes conscious of itself, that is when it may reach up to bring the Light into it. The Gold. The lead must turn to Gold, the coal must turn to Gold, the dust must turn to Gold!"

"How do people come to do things, to know things, and to see things? What is the process that we go through, when headed into a direction, when headed towards a way, a path?"

"That is quite easy to answer! There are two committees within our minds! Both are a set of friends; but one set of friends is the kind that doesn't really believe in you, doesn't encourage you, doesn't coax you into Joy or into Hope. On the contrary, this one set of friends who are on the lefthand side, are there to cast shade upon the tasks at hand, are there to cast doubt upon the directions that you want to take. If you are holding a golden ticket, standing at the entryway to the rest of your life, they are the ones standing on the lefthand side of you who are sneering and jeering and saying to you, 'Do you really think you can make it? Do you really think that you are worth this golden ticket? You won't last twenty minutes once you step outside that door! Why do you think you are holding that ticket in your hand? Do you think you are worthy of it? Because you're not!'

Then on the righthand side of you, there stands the committee of friends who gently echo what you already know in your inner heart of hearts— Joy, Peace, Understanding, Hope, Strength, Courage, Belief, Certainty— they face you with a countenance of certainty, with a serene glow on their faces, and they say to you, 'You know you can do it, you know that this golden ticket is in your hand right now because it is supposed to be there, because you are worth it! You are going to walk out that door, you are going to be happy and brave! You are going to have everything your heart desires, because you can! Because you can! Because you can!' Then in your inner heart of hearts, the voices of your true friends agree with your own voice of knowledge and Wisdom. Because you too, know the things that they say to you, because these things are the truth, you know them, they echo within as the voice of your heart of hearts!"

"So, which way do I go, then? Who do I listen to, then?"

"It may sound like an obvious choice, to go into the direction of the friends who advise you in the way that brings peace to your heart; but the fact is that this is a more difficult process than what it sounds like or looks like. Both of the committees are equally strong and one is ultimately conquered by you adding your own strength to either side (either the lefthand side or the righthand side) and this is easier imagined than done. One committee will pull upon your mind with doubts, fears, the voice that says, 'You must protect yourself from this, because if not, in the end you will look stupid and you will say that we were right!', while the other committee will pull upon your heart and say, 'Remember that the only way you can get to the places you want to go, is if you go towards them and the only way you can go towards them is if you take that first step and the only way to take the first step, is to Believe, is to Trust, is to *know before you know*.' And each group of friends— one on your left and one on your right— will tempt you with equal amounts of strength. You must then add your own strength to either, and that is the side that will conquer."

"How can I add my own weight to the side that believes in me, that finds favour in me, that coaxes me onto the beautiful and brilliant direction?"

"It is truly a duel to the very end, until one side of you is killed. Think it not to be easy! But know that you will be brought to the very ends of your life force, wishing that you would rather die, as your mind and your heart are pulled apart viciously— and finally, perhaps out of exhaustion, you will give in to one or the other."

"But how can I choose the better outcome? You know that I want to choose the righthand side committee! But how can I? Tell me how to, show me how to!"

"You may choose this rigthhand side by looking into the direction that only you and they can see. Others cannot even see it, cannot even understand what you are talking about. Your inner battles are yours to experience and yours to know— far hidden away from what many others around you are capable of comprehending.

Within your inner world, within your Soul, you are still bombarded with the voices of those on the outside, whom you believe would most probably be in favour of the lefthand committee, because of course, they cannot even see any other directions. But then there is you and the righthand side, and you may give your weight to your true group of friends who favour you and who believe in you, by continuing to look into that direction! That direction is *your* direction!

And be not angry with the committee to your left, they are always that way, and will always be that way, have patience with them, and instead, go into the direction opposite of them, with a confident smile and with a confidence and happiness within your heart! Be not angry that they are there! They cannot help themselves! That is just the way that they are!"

"Maybe it would help if I see myself as my own entity, apart from these groups of friends that accompany me in my mind."

"These are not voices in your head, they are not voices speaking to you in your mind; but they are residents of the Country Within, that is your Soul. There are many residents of your Soul. These two groups of friends are there. They are not always with you though, they only show up when you are at a crossroads, at a turning point; creating the necessary friction to propel you into either or direction! The Country Within is not dictated by these friends or these advisors; but they show up to give you your momentum when beginning out on a journey. And let me tell you, let me assure you, that you will never be wrong to go into the direction that confirms the Joy and Peace within your Heart of hearts! Go into the direction that speaks of Favour and Happiness and Courage! Go into the direction that speaks for your worth, the one telling you that *you can*."

"I must know before I know?"

"You must know before you know."

"In this Country Within, is there day and night? Is there Sun and Moon? Is there sky and sea?"

"In my country Within, there is day and night, there is Sun and Moon, and there is sky and sea. There are people of the Moon and people of the Sun, too! The children of the Moon gather on the seashores to contemplate, to brood. They flock to the seashores in unison and they sit on the sand, pondering upon deep meanings and discussing thoughts from the very depths of creation and of everything! The last time I was there, they all held the same book in their hands and they all pondered upon the same pages at the same time, discussing the thoughts there written, with great and true feeling! There is nothing silly about the children of the Moon, nothing funny about them, at all. There is a real Serenity about their countenance, that is lit from within their souls."

"And the children of the Sun? Tell me about them, too!"

"The children of the Sun frolick on the seashores while waters splash and laughter abounds! They have burnt skin and burnt hair and gigantic smiles across their faces! They are Playful, they welcome me in to their Play and I join them, I laugh with them!"

"What do the children of the Moon look like? You didn't mention how they look!"

"Their skin is bathed in Moonlight, their hair is dark and shiny, their eyes are like the seawaters under the Moonshine and they are always brooding, but are also very Serene, they ponder upon mysteries there under the Moon at night."

"What are eyes like seawaters? What does that mean?"

"Have you ever been to the sea at night? The water is dark and reflective of the Moonlight, so it is dark but it is clear, it is not abyssimal, it is actually reflective of the stars and all things that are bright and that are light!"

"Dark eyes that reflect light things!"

"Yes, that is it. Just like the Moon. The Moon is dark, but it is reflective of all things Light, it is therefore Light in the night!"

"And the children of the Sun are always laughing and always burnt under the Sun's rays?"

"Hahahahaha! Yes! That is so! They are Playful and they laugh always, they express their happiness through boisterous play and roudiness! The children of the Moon are equally happy; but the more happy they are, the more that they brood! One could wonder if they are happy or if they are in fact sad— but they are indeed happy. They are in Nirvana, a place of calmness and happiness both at the same time."

"Are they all your friends? Are all of them your friends?"

"They are all my brothers and my sisters, they welcome me into themselves as one of them."

"Both the Sun people and the Moon people do this for you? You are sister to both?"

"Yes, this is true. Why are you surprised? I possess both qualities— both of the Moon and of the Sun. I can be either and I can be both. I can experience Nirvana and I can experience Play! I can experience loud laughter and you already know that I often brood! I am both of these, and alas, I could not have given birth to all of my brothers and my sisters in my Inner Country, if I did not possess the qualities of both!"

"How can you say that you have given birth to your brothers and sisters? This is not possible!"

"We have given birth to all of what is Within! And we have been birthed by them, too! We are born of, and then we conceive of that which we are born! Surely, we are unable to create anything that is not already of us! And surely, nothing can be of us if we were not first created by it!"

"Tell me, please, about the other places within your Country! Are there any other places you think I would like to hear about? I want to know everything, but I know you won't tell me all, but please tell me some more!"

"Why do you think that you know I will not tell you everything?"

"Because, I believe, it is for you to know your own Soul Country, and it is for me to know Mine."

"But aren't I you and aren't you me, aren't we one in the same?"

"If we are one in the same, then why is it that I must ask you these things; shouldn't I already know them?"

"Oh but you do, because I do. I am the you that knows all of the questions that you ask, but you and I are still one in the same, don't you see this?"

"Yes, I do see this."

"When you were small, I visited you often. In your most difficult times, I stood by your side, I was there, I watched over you. I watched you, I comforted you. I was you and you were me, but you couldn't see me, but I could see you and I could feel you. Do you never wonder why you remember being an infant? That time when it was so hot under so many blankets and so many tiny sweaters, that you couldn't breathe? You wanted to tell them to take off your clothes, and to take off the blankets, but you couldn't speak yet? Have you not wondered why you remember that, when you were supposedly too infantile to remember it? And why did you remember it when you were five, then later when you were ten, then now whenever you want to recall it, you remember the very same exact way that you felt in those very same exact moments? It is because I stood by you in those moments, I was there for you, to communicate your need for you. *And I was you!*

From this present moment, I visit that time back then. So, if I remember now, then you remember at five, and then at ten, and then always!

"Have we been doing this always?"

"We have been molding what was, yes, we have been changing the past, through observation— yes. So I will tell you a very significant part of the Soul Country, the Country within you and within me, because you and I are one. I will tell you how there are many temples there, temples that I visit often. Some are new and some are very, very old. Some are polished and some are in ruins. Some are covered by the tides at sea when the Moon is full, while others are on the top of untouchable cliffs! These are temples built for me from time imemorium, until now! I have always had my temples, my palaces, they have always been opulent, I have always been Queen."

"Tell me about the little girl named Selene, and how she pulls at the tides, as if she is the Moon Incarnate."

"I watch over the little girl named Selene, I bring her to my temples, and indeed, she pulls on the seas as if she is the Moon, herself! So we have to very quickly clear the area, before the tides are to rush up and cover everything, entirely! But I am not so sure if Selene is someone else, or if Selene is me! I am not so sure if I have brought the younger me into my

Country and into my temples, to teach her all the things that I know now, or if she is someone else under my ward. We have the same thing, you see, when I step out onto the cliffs, the sea waters rise to meet me! If I so much as think of it, it will rise and swell and come up to touch the skin of my feet! Sometimes it will flow in so strongly and it will flood everything! So I think that Selene is me, and I am teaching her to control the tides, to prevent the floods, because little Selene is too powerful for her own good, and she has a lot to learn if she is to do any good at all with what she has."

"If Selene is you, then Selene is me, too, and you are teaching her as you are teaching me now? You are forming the past, through observation?"

"Yes, that is so."

"Are your temples made of marble?"

"My temples are made of marble, yes, but the older ones are made of heavy stones and rocks, the ones that are now in ruins. They are in ruins because they are ancient, very archaic, they are from times so

long ago, I don't even know how to describe how
ancient they are. Nevertheless, I still visit these
temples and walk out onto the balconies! There are
lion heads carved from stone!"

"Do you ever miss your Home?"

"Yes, I do, I so often do! My Country Within is
my Home. I know where my houses are, where my
temples are, I know the mountains and the
seashores… I know my Home well, and I often miss
it, I sometimes wake in the night and I cry, because
my heart longs for it so. I know the layout of my
Country, I know how to get from one place to
another. I discovered that my dreams were not
random, at all, but all dreams of mine were being
played out in a single Country, where there is a
layout, a map in my mind, I know how to get
anywhere."

"Why are we here on this planet? Why do we
have lives, why do we breathe here and eat here,
why are we here, at all? What is the purpose of it
all?"

"I believe that we traverse this Earth, to find the missing materials that we need for building our eternal homes in the world that is adjacent to this one. Adjacent and unseen, but not undetectable. But then during our lives here, we also utilise materials from our eternal space for using as we build our lives here in our corporeal space. It is a give-and-take relationship. A give-and-take relationship between our bodies and our souls, between our minds and our spirits. There are materials here that are needed there and those are what we harvest whilst being here. But there are also many materials there that are needed here and those are what we pull into our lives while we are here.

I of course do not think that this is being done by everybody, but I believe that this is being done by some. Some know this is what they are doing, while others later on realise this is what they have been doing all along.

'Heaven' is actually a country that we build within ourselves, or that we continue to build. We come from it, and we harvest materials for it while we are here, doing this through sharing our talents with others, and through being dedicated to our relationships in life, through loving others and through strengthening our ability to believe, through our Faith. What is Faith? Faith is the strength to believe even when believing is a very difficult thing to do! I think that Faith is acquired here in this world, because there is no need to have Faith in our Eternal Countries. But here, as we acquire Faith in the midst of our hardships, we are begetting unto our Eternal Countries the strong glue that holds some buildings and some temples together. It is all for the adjacent world that we do this. And yet, we may bring that world into this one, just the same as our voices are the sounds of our souls speaking through our throats; so are our eternal cities and eternal colours the breath that we breathe while in this life. And sometimes, breath materialises in condensation, and even more, in snow! It can be real. All of it can be real. We need not be limited by physical matter; but we may choose what to make into physical matter. We may choose our realities, mould them, create them, cause them to bloom in front of our eyes.

I believe that we are not determined either to Heaven or to Hell, through our actions here on

Earth. On the contrary, I believe that we come either from Heaven or from Hell, prior to this life, and we carry our prior origins inside of us, at all times. Then we are responsible for bringing either Heaven or Hell into this world, in our own small and big ways. Then, we just go back to where we originally came from. And we live in this life as a result of where we once were.

Of course, we do have the capacities to develop and to build and to create more, while we are here, and perhaps even to change the course of our destinies, but I believe that the soul matter of individuals are varied and are not of all the same origins.

Perhaps a human simply falls back into himself upon the disintegration of his physical body and continues to take form within the self of himself, simply returning from whence he came."

"All this talk of Self... does this mean that all eternal purpose and all eternal reason is unto Self and about Self and with Self and for Self?"

"There is a downfall that happens when the focus of anything becomes self-centered. Look at the modern-day organisations of this world, even the ones that hail from the archaic schools of Divinity and Theosophy; they have become communities that are looking out for their own interests, looking out for how they are perceived. The downfall begins when the attitude turns from, 'I am in this world and I am meant to do something in it, I am meant to traverse it, I am meant to discover it and discover things and living beings in it and I am meant to do good and to have good, and I am meant to know what this is and what this means and who they are and what their meaning is', into one of, 'This world and all of the living beings in it must see me as this and must see me like this because this is how I should be seen as, because I am here for a reason and everyone needs to know that, everyone needs to discover me.' To the naked eye, it is almost the same thing, it is a subtle shift. But to the one who Sees— this is a profound shift that makes the difference between Heaven and Earth!

I am here for a purpose and I appreciate this world and this Earth; therefore, I must discover it, because as I discover it and as I discover you in it— my own story will reveal itself to me. *That* is the mindset that is going to *prevent* a collapse into oneself. And when I say 'collapse into one's self' I do not mean like a collapsing star; rather, I mean a disintegration. Greatness ends where self-centeredness begins.

I guess you can call it a paradox— the fact that the ultimate journey is the journey to know oneself, to take the inward path into oneself, and yet, self-centredness is the defeat of that very same inward journey! But there is a piece that people are missing and I want to show you that piece to this puzzle. You see, there are three parts of the Self. There is your outer shell, which is of course your body; there is your ego self; which is the one that will have you falling into self-centredness if you are not aware; then there is your True Self that is everlasting, the one we call *Soul*. There can be no self-centredness on the journey within Soul, because within Soul, no selfishness exists. You journey through the Country that thrives within your inner lands and there is nothing selfish or moronic about journeying through, and discovering, a country! It is a country unseen, I already explained that earlier. This is the neverending journey of Soul, of You; this is not ego, this has nothing to do with the preoccupation of how you are perceived or how you present yourself to anyone or to the whole world!

Soul must honour Flesh and Flesh must honour Soul. So, it is your outermost and your innermost faculties that must come together, love one another, and work with one another. This is the true Love of Self. This is the true act of falling in love with oneself.

Narcissism is not Love of the Self; on the contrary, narcissism is the preoccupation with the ego— with the part of the self that is in between the innermost and the outermost parts of you. And it is not a love. No one should use the word 'love' to term something which does not produce anything beautiful. The narcissist is preoccupied with the presentation of the faculty that is easily reactive, easily provoked, self-absorbed and insatiably self-gratifying. But this has nothing to do with Love, not at all. The nacrissist does not Love himself; the narcissist *does not know himself*.

We are born into this world and the first things that we learn are our reflections in the mirrors— a physical form of self-awareness. We learn that our hands are there, existing at the ends of our arms; we learn that our feet are down there, existing at the ends of our legs; we gain an awareness of ourselves in relation to the space around us. This is all physical and this is okay. But it is the connection between this outermost faculty and our innermost faculty that is the key to Enlightenment and Awareness, that is the key to Freedom and Truth.

The problem that arises with many people, happens when they become stuck upon the middle faculty— the ego— they fail to discover the inner faculty and their sense of awareness becomes a loop, a cycle, of outer and middle stimulation; of physical and egotistical stimuli. The funny thing is that ego will always try to be equated to Soul, it will say, 'I am in the spirit, I am in this sort of kindness, I am in this sort of awareness, I am in this sort of awakening, I am enlightened and unburdened and I follow the Dalai Lama and I am all about energies and spiritual roots and all that jazz. I'm on top in this way, my spirit is in tip top shape, I don't understand why other people can't be like this, why can't other people get over their darkness like I have? They must be weak or they must be dumb.' This is the dialogue of ego, the one who wants to relate itself to Soul.

As a matter of fact, ego is not Soul and Soul will overcome ego. Or, it *should* overcome ego. It is not within Soul where the wild beasts are found; but it is within ego. Soul must conquer and victor over these beasts in the dark chambers of ego, thus bridging the gap between Flesh and the ultimate Inner Self."

"But I have a question... does not the ego strengthen you, make you braver and stronger? Does not the ego act as the cement between body and Soul?"

"Nay, the ego is the one who weakens you, keeps you from your Destiny, keeps you from going beyond! Your ego is the one that weakens you from doing what you really want, because attached to the thing that you really want, is the possibility of not achieving it or the possibility of losing it. Fear of your plans not going your way is the doing of ego. The hesitation you fear that something may not go as you planned it, is also the doing of ego. Because it is the ego which will fall if you do not attain what you desire, or if you lose what you desire. Your Soul will not fall to that, your body will not fall to that— but your ego will! Your ego therefore is oftentimes able to keep you away from the thing that you want the most! Would you call that Strength? Would you call that Courage? I really don't think so!"

"Tell me all about the importance of language, of words. Some men speak seven languages, while others speak only one. How does this fair to or against the value of a man?"

"The number of languages spoken means nothing. If you speak ten languages and I speak only a single word, yet with this one word, I am able to bring life to the dead and to cause these rocks right here to breathe— what then is the value of your ten languages against the value of my single word? People have become so preoccupied in the ways that they are seen rather than preoccupied in the ways of the Divine— in bringing the dead to life and causing rocks to breathe. There are those so preoccupied with how they are seen on the surface, that they have lost all of their roots underneath the ground! A rootless rose is a dead rose. A rootless tree is a dead tree."

"But why do you call this a preoccupation with the surface of things?"

"Because people have lost the meaning of words, of language. In a single word, the dead can be brought to life and the rocks can begin to breathe! But who knows this? Who knows these things? Who can call the storms to a standstill, who can call forth the Sun to light a new day, who can smear the Moon from the sky with a word? They could— and yet they can't. They don't know what they could do, because they are so preoccupied with what is in front of their eyes, and that is, the concern with others and others' opinions about them. To say that you can speak many languages is a great accomplishment for them. But with a single sentence, I can do in the hearts of men, what they cannot do in the hearts of men in all of their lives, even with all their learned languages put together! Surely you agree that if I know but a single word, and yet this single word may cause the dead to rise, this is far better than to know ten languages but not be able to affect a heartbeat, to affect the breath?"

"I surely know this, I cannot imagine any man who would not agree with this."

"And yet there are those who would not agree with this, because they know nothing more than what they already know. The number of languages that a person speaks does not matter. What matters is what a person can do with even a single language. Even someone deaf and mute may be able to shake the world harder and longer than someone else who can speak. And that is because it is not through language that we communicate, but, it is through Heart."

"Do they want to know more?"

"Some want to know more but will never seek it, some want to know more and will seek it but not find it, and others want to know more and they will seek it and they will find it. As you have."

The Creed of Venusta

I. When you receive an act of kindness from another person, plant this kindness given to you as one would plant a seed in the fertile soil of one's garden. Return to it again and again, attend to it again and again, water that plant; repay the kind giver for the act of kindness, over and over again. Never forget a kindness given to you, and for as long as that person has pure intention towards you, repay that person for their act, with your own actions of value and pure intention.

II. When you gather around your table to celebrate good things, remember those who helped to bring you the bounty that you eat; whether they be Higher Powers Unseen, loved ones, friends, the animals that protect and provide, or the trees and plants that supply us with life. They have given to you, they have given to your table; be thankful as you feast.

III. Many are those who will not help you if you fall. And many are those who will not celebrate with you as you rise. Remember who they are, your time is better not wasted on them. One day they will fall and one day they will rise; neither requires your attention.

I hope
you have
enjoyed this book
my darling girl ♡
share the Love :)
Ale xxx

Special Mentions

First and foremost, I would like to thank my copyeditor and friend, Toula Fanariotou of Thessaloniki in Greece, for editing my manuscript like nobody else can. I ponder upon this sometimes, I think it's remarkable how a native Greek speaker is the editor of my English works. Once upon a time, I used to be brought to the brink of calamity every time I published a book. It's so strenuous to edit your own work over and over again (one must make a larger margin for error when editing one's own work). I would have to go over my work three times just to remove flaws, and still, I would find remaining mistakes after the book was already published. Martha Graham, the influential modern-day dancer and choreographer hailed as the Picasso of dance and choreography, once said, "You see, when weaving a blanket, an Indian woman leaves a flaw in the weaving of that blanket to let the soul out." I believe in this saying and I have always applied it to my manuscripts. I will intentionally leave a flaw in my manuscripts, leave it just the way it is, in order to let the soul out. And it is my way of loving the manuscript just the way it is without demanding of it to be perfect. Yes, I really apply this principle to my manuscripts, I am not even joking in the least. However, this still does not mean that I don't work to make the manuscript as flawless as possible. This is why I am grateful for my friend Toula, who is now here to help me achieve that.

There is something profound about having a Greek person edit your work. Greece, afterall, is the birthplace of profundity in language (from my own angle of being an English speaker). Having a Greek woman as a copyeditor means that she is able to understand the esoteric soul within my written words, so she's not going to edit out what's supposed to be in there and she's not going to add any extra words or even just punctuations if she feels that they won't benefit the very essence of my words.

I'm also feeling very grateful for the positive collaboration on the book cover design. Jim Crotty has been a long-time supporter of my work so when it was time to find a photographer, it was easy for him to get my vision. He spent his own money purchasing flower variety after flower variety until we finally got it right! I knew from the beginning that I wanted roses but we needed another kind of flower to symbolise the other half, so it was a period of trial and error.

I am also thankful to everyone who submitted their photos for consideration, I am thankful for their time, their energy and eagerness to work with me.

I'm so thankful to have been accompanied on this journey of publication by a panel of individuals whom I truly admire and who truly amaze me! My Beta Readers form an egalitarian team comprised of highly accomplished individuals who have made powerful and unique choices in their lives which have propelled them forward into the direction of their goals and dreams. Nobody was friends with anybody else before joining my team; but now we are all a part of this small but mighty army of friends.

The journey that has come about from this collaboration with my Beta Readers, is a journey far more positive than I imagined it could be. In the Introduction to this book, I mentioned my anxiety about publishing this conversation, but it is in the feedback from the Beta Readers that I have found my solace, comfort, and empowerment. Long-forgotten broken pieces within me have been mended, healed, rebuilt; I remember those pieces once again when I feel them healing, as I read the reviews from those I invited to be the first readers of this work. I have healed and guided many others through this conversation and my reward is one that I didn't even know to ask for! For this, I thank the Greater Powers that be.

I want to thank *you*— the one holding this book in your hands. I want to thank everyone who has shared my work with friends and family, who has spread my words out into the world. Thank you for being my messengers.

Information on the Photographer:
Jim Crotty, Photography by Jim Crotty LLC,
jimcrotty.zenfolio.com

The main typeface in this book is set in 12 pt. *Perpetua*, by Eric Gill (1882- 1940), who was a British sculptor and stonecutter named *Royal Designer for Industry* by the *Royal Society of Arts* in London. The font itself was crafted in such a way to resemble hand-chiseled engravings, hence, who better to create such a feel for a font, than a sculptor and stonecutter?

"Perpetua may be judged in the small sizes to have achieved the object of providing a distinguished form for a distinguished text; and, in the large sizes, a noble, monumental appearance."
~ Stanley Morison

Printed in Poland
by Amazon Fulfillment
Poland Sp. z o.o., Wrocław